I0453833

Praise for *The Quest for Happily Ever After*

"Dan led the marriage ministry for fourteen years at The Rock Church in Castle Rock, Colorado. The weekend church attendance at that time averaged about fifteen hundred people. He and his wife Linda developed and taught marriage training manuals and retreats with their original curriculum. They regularly taught classes of twenty to forty people and retreats of fifty to a hundred people. Dan was licensed by The Rock Church as the marriage pastor.

Dan's passion for empowering marriage comes through on every page. He and his wife are vulnerable and transparent as they share their struggles and triumphs. They walk with you on the quest of building a connected marriage and securing a healthy sexual identity.

This book is sure to take you into a place of healing for deeper heart issues. We encounter Jesus there where transformation begins."

—J.R. Polhemus, senior pastor of
The Rock Church, 1988–2017, Castle Rock, Colorado

* * *

"A creative, intelligent, and deep-hearted take on the pursuit of the marriage we dream of — in the Eldredge tradition."

—Peter Lundell, D. Miss., former missionary,
pastor, and author of *Prayer Power,
Armed for Battle, and Short Stories for the Soul*

"An insightful pastor and writer, Dan Lillyblad does a fine job in guiding spouses into more personal wholeness. His experience—cultivated over forty years—makes this a great read for all marrieds seeking deepening in marital commitment."

— Andrew Comiskey, founding director of
Desert Stream Ministries

The Quest

for

Happily Ever After

Creating Authentic Intimacy in Marriage

Daniel F. Lillyblad

The Quest for Happily Ever After
Copyright © 2025 by Daniel F. Lillyblad

All rights reserved. No part of this book may be reproduced in any form or by any means — whether electronic, digital, mechanical, or otherwise — without permission in writing from the publisher, except by a reviewer, who may quote brief passages in a review.

Scripture quotations marked NKJV are taken from the New King James Version®. Copyright © 1982 by Thomas Nelson. Used by permission. All rights reserved. Scripture quotations marked NIV are taken from the Holy Bible, New International Version®, NIV® Copyright ©1973, 1978, 1984, 2011 by Biblica, Inc.® Used by permission. All rights reserved worldwide. Scripture quotations marked NLT are taken from the Holy Bible, New Living Translation, copyright © 1996, 2004, 2015 by Tyndale House Foundation. Used by permission of Tyndale House Publishers, Inc., Carol Stream, Illinois 60188. All rights reserved. Scriptures marked (ERV) are taken from the HOLY BIBLE: EASY-TO-READ VERSION © 2014 by Bible League International. Used by permission. Scripture quotations marked ESV are taken from the Holy Bible, English Standard Version. ESV® Text Edition: 2016. Copyright © 2001 by Crossway Bibles, a publishing ministry of Good News Publishers. Scripture quotations marked NIV are taken from the Holy Bible, New International Version®, NIV® Copyright ©1973, 1978, 1984, 2011 by Biblica, Inc.® Used by permission. All rights reserved worldwide. Scripture quotations marked MSG are taken from The Message Copyright © 1993, 2002, 2018 by Eugene H. Peterson. Scripture quotations marked RSV are taken from the Revised Standard Version of the Bible, copyright © 1946, 1952, and 1971 the Division of Christian Education of the National Council of the Churches of Christ in the United States of America. Used by permission. All rights reserved.

The views and opinions expressed in this book are those of the author and do not necessarily reflect the official policy or position of Illumify Media Global.

Published by
Illumify Media Global
www.IllumifyMedia.com
"Let's bring your book to life!"

Library of Congress Control Number: 2024925110

Paperback ISBN: 978-1-964251-62-2

Typeset by Art Innovations (http://artinnovations.in/)
Cover design by Debbie Lewis

Printed in the United States of America

*It simply isn't an adventure worth
telling if there aren't any dragons.*

—J.R.R. Tolkien

Dedication

I dedicate this book to Linda, my wife and life companion, lover, and best friend. Thank you for taking this journey of faith with me and for the patience, love, and support I always find in your presence. Thank you for believing.

This book is also for those looking for love and those who haven't been able to make love work for them — and maybe have given up hoping for a happily ever after. You who have reached for love and have been brokenhearted are the ones who fuel the passion for this writing. May you find beauty for ashes. This was written for you. God loves you, there is hope, and anything can change and get better. Try to look up, take a deep breath, and find the courage to believe again. My prayer is that wisdom will come to those needing it — that you will find a key or two that will open locked doors of relating in your life and marriage.

I pray you will see yourself in the stories, examples, and strategies given, and will know what to do to make things different. My prayers and faith go with God's Word of healing for your lives. The fruit is in the seed. God's word doesn't return empty, and our redeemer is mighty.

Contents

Acknowledgments xi

Introduction 1

1. Someday My Prince Will Come 3

2. Life in Separate Towers 15

3. The Curse of Stolen Identity 29

4. Invite the Hero of Your Story into Your Quest 42

5. Secure the Castle 58

6. Win the Power Challenge 76

7. Break the Curse of "Me" over "We" 98

8. Banish Shame 110

9. Heal Your Sexuality 123

10. Escape from Idolatry 142

11. Banish the Differences Myth 168

12. Wield Words Well 184

13. Break the Chains of Dysfunctional Relationships 195

14. Celebrate the Gift of Sexuality 206

15. Be a Freedom Fighter..223

16. The Road Home..240

Study Guide for the Quest..246

State of the Union Evaluation 249

Rules of Engagement Covenant..................................258

Notes 273

Acknowledgments

I want to thank first the one I follow—Jesus, the Good Shepherd—whom I seek to follow in all things. Thank you for your guidance, wisdom, and revelation. Each time this book stopped in its tracks, I stopped with it, turned to you, and waited for your pace, process, and direction. I know I wrote this book, but it's all yours and so is all the glory for it.

Every good and perfect gift is from him. We are told to earnestly desire the best gifts, and the best are those offered in love to the ones who need them most—then their joy becomes ours.

I also thank Illumify Media who helped make this book possible. I couldn't have finished without all of you. Surely God has put you in my path. Thank you, Mike Klassen, for your patience and friendship as I have found my way, and for the leadership you continue to provide to the writing community. Thank you, Karen Bouchard, for the coaching, editing, and guidance in helping me write, mostly for believing in me and not letting me quit. Thank you also, Jen Clark, for your gift of organization that doesn't go unnoticed, and Geoff Stone and Deb Hall who helped with copyediting and putting it all together at the end. And I thank Debbie Lewis for the beautiful book cover.

My thanks also to the mentors and influencers who have befriended me and helped me along the way. None of us can do it alone. Thank you.

"The LORD has established his throne in heaven, and His kingdom rules over all" (Psalm 103:19).

Introduction

Whether you're contemplating marriage and want to be prepared, or whether you've already said "I do" and are facing challenges you didn't expect, welcome to the quest for happily ever after.

Few adventures in life are what we thought before we embarked, and marriage is no exception. No one starts with all the answers, and those who think so are soon humbled when they realize that love is asking for more than they have.

This book starts with expectations and honeymoon love, then explores the emotional reality of disillusionment and its challenges. I chose the storybook fairy-tale theme because, that's exactly what marriage can feel like, right? It encompasses love's enchantment, thrills, challenges, dragons, dark forests, courage, and more.

Unlike fairy tales, deep heart issues don't go away with the wave of a fairy godmother's wand. It takes time in God's healing presence to see ourselves and to respond to his love before we truly have what it takes to love and be loved in our marriages.

This is because our hearts need healing so they can love. We can't risk love at the level needed for connection and intimacy with the baggage we carry to the altar from home and our histories. This needs unpacking in a safe and healing environment. This book was created to show that environment. Our Redeemer Jesus is mighty, and He calls Himself the Good Shepherd. He came and gave all to heal the brokenhearted and set the captives free. He's on a mission to seek and save our hearts. All who call upon his name are saved, healed, and delivered—but it's a journey and a healing process that takes work, warfare, and a surrendered heart.

The Bible says that "all we like sheep have gone astray" (Isa. 53:6). I see married strugglers as sheep who've lost their way and just need some help getting back on the path. They need someone like Jesus, the hero of our story, who leaves the ninety-nine, finds them, throws them over his shoulders, and brings them back to the Father's house for some healing ministry.

My prayer is that you will have encounters with God as you move through the book. Wait on his timing, ask for the Holy Spirit, and let him speak to you. He will show you how to build the bridges and connections that will lead you both deeper into each other's hearts.

I put connection questions, tools, and exercises into a study guide at the end of the book that includes things you can work on. Try to do these things together if you can—and if your spouse doesn't engage, do them yourself. You will still benefit from this journey and find healing.

I am praying for you as you embark on this adventure.

You really *can* experience happily ever after.

XO,

Dan

Chapter One
Someday My Prince Will Come

*I've been dreaming of a true love's kiss, and a prince I'm hoping
comes with this.*
—"True Love's Kiss" from the Disney movie *Enchanted*

The first time I saw the phrase "Someday my prince will come," it was on a wooden plaque on the office door of Danielle, our church administrator. Beneath the words sat a cartoonish frog with a crooked crown on his head.

That sign represented much more than a cute saying: it embodied hope for happily ever after, a long-awaited fairy-tale union that would break the spell that was keeping love and companionship at bay. *Once this spell is broken by my new lover, I'll never be lonely and find what's been missing for so long.*

I knew a bit of Danielle's story. After a twenty-year marriage fell apart, she had rebuilt her life but was still hoping for a relationship where she could experience true love and live happily ever after.

Being a romantic, I hoped Danielle's prince would come. And he did! Robert was a handsome, quiet friend she had known since high school. After graduation, he got married and stayed in their rural hometown to work the family farm. When he lost his wife to illness, he, too, was hoping for another chance at love.

They rekindled their friendship and spent months getting to know each other on a deeper level until *voilà*! My wife, Linda, and I witnessed their happy wedding as their new journey began.

After their wedding, they moved back to Nebraska, and we lost touch with them. But if I know anything at all about love and relationships, I know this: the quest for happily ever after doesn't end with wedding vows—that's when it begins.

What We Long for versus What We Get

A "Someday my prince [or princess] will come" sign has hung over most of our hearts—and maybe still does. After all, who doesn't long for love? Even if we're not sure what that's supposed to look like, we believe when we find it, things will be different and better. We hope the prince or princess of our dreams will provide everything we long for. In fact, we're counting on it!

When we initially marry, we feel like wild horses on an unlimited range. Like Adam and Eve in the pristine, steamy garden, we are naked and unashamed, with access to all the love and positive emotions we'll ever need. We say to ourselves in gratitude, *Finally, my partner is here to 'love me to life'!*

She thinks, *Now I won't be alone anymore. We'll be connected on this exciting adventure! We will dream, plan, and do life together. I'll love our long talks as he lives out my dreams with me.*

He thinks, *Now I have access to sexual fulfillment and companionship. She will come with me on all my adventures. I'll show her how to hunt and fish and ride a motorcycle. She'll love the things I do and live out my dreams with me.*

Sadly, it doesn't take long for our idealistic honeymoon feelings to start fading. We can feel cheated, as the energy of our different desires and needs begin to compete. Where did that power struggle and tension come from? We fear we've lost what we had and it will never come back.

We haven't lost love, per se, but love as we imagined it, and we have active imaginations. We've lost our blindness to the faults of our partner, and what we now see has dimmed our sense of intimate connection. It's clear they are unable to bring us what we expect or need, and the pain makes us pull back.

We didn't even know the magnitude of what we were expecting until we started hurting. We didn't hurt until we were next to someone who could give us what we needed but wouldn't or couldn't. Before long, we feel a painful distance between how we thought it would be, and the way things are shaking out. We feel set up because "love" promised us lots of things but can't seem to deliver.

Something else begins to happen after the honeymoon glow dims. Not only are they not meeting all our needs, but we see our own flaws more clearly and feel our inability to give our beloved all *they* expect and want. We declared at the altar what we truly meant to bring to our partner, but now it's harder and harder to come through. We thought we knew how to please them, but now it's not so clear. We think to ourselves, *I thought this would be so different.*

As the dynamics change and the lawn dries out, our fields of gold begin showing patches of crabgrass. Before long, as our Eden slips away, we find ourselves looking for fig leaves to cover the exposure we feel. We begin withholding from each other as we feel insecure, exposed, and unsure. It helps to know that this is quite normal.

What Goes Wrong?

Why doesn't marriage usher us immediately and irrevocably into the land of happily ever after? In the words of C.S. Lewis, "Eros is driven to promise what Eros of himself cannot perform. Can we be in this selfless liberation for a lifetime? Hardly for a week."[1]

Think of honeymoon love (aka eros, or erotic love) as the booster rockets that get the ship off the ground. We think our love intensity will last forever, but the fuel of eros love will always fade.

Eros burns away fast to reveal the authentic players in the marriage. Who I *thought* you were turned into who you *truly* are. The full strength of our expectations is only seen as we begin to experience our marriage partners for who they really are. There are new adjustments to this reality needed in our thinking and emotions, and it hurts.

Now we need new fuel to keep the rocket going "till death do us part."

In other words, we signed up for connection/romance/sex/companionship. We didn't know it would take self-sacrifice, character development, and a redefinition of what we thought marriage was all about.

Who knew transformation was on the table?

In John and Stasi Eldredge's book *Love and War*, the authors offer this:

- Marriage is a divine conspiracy; it is a conspiracy divinely arranged and with divine intent. God lures us into marriage through love, and sex, and loneliness. He lures us into marriage and then he uses it to transform us.
- Come back to the fairy tales—in every one of those stories, the boy and the girl each carry a fatal flaw. If they refuse their transformation—which is essential to the plot of the story—they'll never make it.
- Evil will win, they will lose heart and split up, and there will be no happily ever after. In Beauty and the Beast, Beauty is a prima donna, and the Beast has anger management issues. She must find her courage and he must find his tenderness.
- In every one of these stories, happily ever after waits upon a particular turn of events, at the center of which is the character's transformation.[2]

Slowly, we begin to understand the personal cost of completing the quest for our wholeness and marital oneness. We didn't think we'd have to work this hard to be married and in love. Now, instead of unifying and living happily ever after in a united kingdom built together, we find ourselves retreating to our divided towers.

In our towers of self-protection, we blame our spouses for the loss of our fairy-tale fantasies and focus on how we can change them. We can go into denial of our relational realities and tell ourselves that our "dreams" can be saved if we make the "necessary changes" to our partner. We find ourselves holding back and may even begin plotting how we can establish our power base. (*After all,* we think, *someone's gotta be in charge; we better get that established up front.*)

The controlling tendencies we possess that were dormant during the infatuation stage kick in. We may try to manipulate our partner to perform a certain way so we can maintain the feeling of being "in love."

No wonder conflict emerges.

Let God Search and Know Your Heart

To reclaim our lost identities and become whole, we must invite God into the process of learning who we are, our true selves. Only then can he help us become aware of our damaging patterns of intimacy and replace them with life-giving ones. The psalmist David wrote these words to God:

"Search me O God, and know my heart; Try me, and know my anxieties. And see if there is any wicked way in me, and lead me in the way everlasting" (Ps. 139:23–24).

In other words, our identity—and our search to fill the deepest longings of our hearts—doesn't start by focusing on our spouses and how we can change them.

It begins with our relationship with God and how he might change *us*.

The psalmist says, "You have searched me and known me" (Ps. 139:1).

At its best, self-awareness is intimacy with God as he shows us to ourselves. We may not be accustomed to this level of intimacy as we are unaware of our inner selves and the patterns that originate there. The intimacy our souls long for is found in this love relationship with God. Here, our identity and security needs are met. The curse of stolen identity is broken, and we are reunited with our true selves. We are no longer haunted by loneliness and a disconnected soul, seeking relief.

When we invite God to show us who we are and how we relate, we become self-aware of our dynamics and responses. These revelations are transformational when we act upon what we see: *Oh, that's what I'm doing that's causing this reaction from her, or him— I can change that; I don't have to do that or be that way. This isn't helping me or us anyway. I can let that go.*

Marriages can't live and grow if the partners are unable to see their wounds, wrong beliefs, or broken patterns and what they do to each other. This is because deeper intimacy isn't possible between two unaware individuals.

Self-awareness helps you identify these unhealthy responses. Without self-awareness we cling to our denial believing, *They're the problem, not me,* rather than, *Wow, that's what I do that's causing this.* Your marriage improves when you see the hurtful things you are doing to each other and choose to stop doing them.

I liken self-awareness to a pair of corrective lenses bringing truth that shows you who you are. Like reading glasses, things are fuzzy until you put them on, then you have twenty-twenty vision *into yourself.* It shows you the real you and how your personality affects your spouse. We begin discerning our dynamics with God's wisdom.

Without the ability to see me as she does, I stay my defensive self and crash down the road in an insensitive manner, unaware of the hurt I am causing. Our only salvation is humbly allowing our spouse to show and tell us what we're doing and how it affects them. We will secure the castle in chapter 5, making it safe to do this.

When Jesus knocks on the door, we respond by opening it (Rev. 3:20). He leads and guides us into the truth only as we let him (John 16:13). He gives us the power to *become* as we choose light and truth. Self-awareness helps you own who you are and grow, instead of hiding and blaming. This is hard at first, then easier as you gain awareness of the relational and spiritual benefits of "seeing." This process heals us—and in the process, our marriage is healed as well.

It's been said that self-awareness is curative if a person will be humble and honest about what they see. It can also empower us to make responsible choices about what we find. I can think to myself, *I don't have to be that way about this. I can change that. I can see this is not loving and how it hurts you and us; it has to go.*

We connect and feel better as the negative patterns fall away, along with the bad emotions that surround them. Love makes these choices, deciding we don't want pain and brokenness, but wholeness and connection. Love teaches us to connect by honoring and valuing our spouses rather than disconnecting from the process through avoidance. This is loving each other to life. I can say to myself, or tell her, *I'm going to press into this with you because I love you. It's painful and I don't understand the dynamics, but I want a connection with you so I'm in.*

This is hopeful, because when you can see what you are doing and why, you can then choose to do something about it. Understanding and awareness bring hope, and our pain and suffering are lessened as we remove hurtful dynamics. Confusion leaves once we see what we're doing and understand the consequences of our actions. We are the architects and really can make our marriages feel better!

Self-awareness brings us hope as we

- gain wisdom for the process and become empowered (Prov. 24:3),
- discover who we are in the marriage (find ourselves),
- gain insights into the cause and effect of our unique related dynamics,
- see what we are doing to each other, and why, take ownership of it, and
- start growing into mature, unselfish loving.

Breaking the Spells of the Two Towers

Thanks to fairy tales and Disney movies, we get the idea that, like Snow White or Sleeping Beauty, women can fall under a spell and look to their prince to break that spell. In the typical quest, the princess is locked in a tower under a spell of some kind, and the prince's role is to come and rescue her.

But here's what many of us don't realize: guys are under a spell too. Remember the frog prince? He was under a spell, needing transformation. Beauty's Beast also had problems.

In other words, both princes and princesses are dealing with their isolation and baggage, locked in their unique personality towers that prevent them from becoming one. The primary characteristic of the tower is that it hastens our retreat into isolation and prevents our bonding. Our towers, and how we behave when we are in them, are the enemy of intimacy and connection. In our brokenness, we do things that prevent connection and sabotage intimacy. These are the broken patterns of relating we will discover.

Our healing journey, or quest, is the path out of lonely separation into wholeness. It's a process that leads to marital oneness, agreement, and fulfillment. This is the path of transformation and spiritual growth. As we yield to God and stay on the path, we become whole, confident, and enabled to love and give our hearts to each other.

God doesn't give the gift of marriage for us to be unhappy, lonely, or frustrated. He gives us the invitations and clues we need if we seek him and trust him as our Healer. He wants us to be one and to find joy in our marriages. This is his will for us.

Research shows that these relational towers are gender specific. The prince is trapped in the kind of emotional tower specific to his typically masculine struggles. The princess is locked in an emotional tower unique to her struggles with womanhood.

Studying the two towers is not intended to pigeonhole the sexes or generalize their traits. For example, in our marriage, as a male, I'm more emotional, do most of the cooking, and love to discuss feelings. Linda is more analytical, takes care of the finances, arranges travel plans, and must work to stay engaged in the "feelings" talks I initiate. We have learned to honor (and be grateful for) each other's strengths. It takes time.

Your relationship dance is unique, and one you must discover together. The spells we're under, and the brokenness we bring into our marriages are often rooted in wounds common to our birth gender. The more these wounds are made whole, the more we can function in whole roles as God intended.

By the way, marriage doesn't put us in our separate towers: we come into the marriage already locked in them; we could say that marriage makes them visible by exposing us. Marriage doesn't turn us into someone else after we say, "I do." Who we are and how we act relationally shows up center stage. The stairsteps leading to our towers are our unmet needs, histories, sins, and brokenness. The locks and chains keeping us there are the unhealthy patterns of relating we've learned and reinforced throughout our lives. Most of us have grown up as survivors and have known no other way.

The interesting thing is we don't even realize how isolated we are in our towers, what put us there, and what's keeping us there, until we hook up with our spouses and begin finding out, as they reflect our true selves to us, and my, is *that* awkward.

Marriage doesn't *make us* who we are; it *reveals* who we are. It's when we build our marriage castle that the towers show up. Marriage is God's stage that reveals who the main characters are. Finally, you get to be center stage. As we will see, this is love's bid for our transformation, and we will find there is a cross in the theater.

We thought marriage was going to be the answer, the way *out* of the tower. But getting married isn't the answer to who we are; it only changes the scenery. We thought marriage would be our Eden, and we would enjoy slices of it, but for now, it feels more like a war zone. We're about to find out who we are.

Let the Quest Begin

In any good fairy tale, before the prince and princess can live happily ever after, there are obstacles to face, enchantments to break, and dragons to slay.

Your marriage is no different.

And yet overcoming the obstacles, breaking the curses, and slaying the dragons are the very things that transform us into the partners and lovers we've always dreamed of being—the very things that transform our marriage into something worth fighting for.

We *can* get to "happily ever after." But it doesn't arrive when we say, "I do." We begin to experience it—fleetingly, often, and eventually daily—as we embrace the adventure of facing the challenges, curses, and dragons together.

CHAPTER TWO
Life in Separate Towers

Under the weight of competing priorities, we often feel like passing couriers who can only wave and wish the other well. . . . We hope that somehow life tomorrow will enable us to do what we cannot do today.

—Dan Allender

The first challenge we must overcome on our journey to happily ever after is a big one, a trifecta of brokenness, unrealistic expectations, and idolatry.

Our brokenness hinders us from meeting the needs of our spouses; we don't know what they are. At the same time, we place unrealistic expectations on our spouses to meet all our needs (becoming hurt and disillusioned in the process). Finally, in looking to our spouses for salvation, we misplace our worship, forgetting that our deepest needs can only be satisfied by God and not by the people in our lives.

And here's the biggest part of the challenge: we don't even realize we're facing these things. We don't know what separates us and why we can't connect. This contributes to our disillusionment and confusion.

The alarming result is that, instead of finding the happily ever after for which we long, we and our spouses find ourselves locked in separate towers, lonely and frustrated.

Healing the Wound

The first step to unlocking our towers and finding a connection is to identify the wound at the root of our pain and isolation. This wound is an attack on our gender identity (who we are as men and women), an attack that lies to us and steals our whole identity as male or female. We will unpack this in the next chapter.

The truth is that the wound (or curse) created by Adam and Eve's fall in the garden is still working against men and women today.

In the garden of Eden, God created man and woman to be in fellowship with each other and with Him. When Satan tricked Eve into doubting God and choosing her own reasoning over God's instructions to her, she (and subsequently Adam) felt conflict in their relationship with each other and separation from God.

The enemy brought the sword between the sexes. After all, Adam not only blamed Eve for giving him the fruit but even blamed God for giving him Eve in the first place!

The man said, "The woman you put here with me—she gave me some fruit from the tree, and I ate it" (Gen. 3:12 NIV).

In other words, empowered men and women with authority suddenly became victims who could no longer take responsibility and love, but now only blamed and tried to control.

This wound of sin is at the root of the feeling we all struggle with, the one that tells us, *I'm not enough.* It's at the root of our hunger for assurance, acceptance, and validation. It leaves us craving connection with each other and God, while at the same time rendering us unable to create the connection we so desire. Only with God's help can we find and remove the things within that sabotage love and connection. Let's look at the two towers.

Her Life in the Tower

For women, the struggle with feelings of inadequacy is painful and real. The self-doubt and lies sent by Satan, society, and even people who are supposed to care for her are real.

The devil's lie to women cuts to the core of their femininity. He knows if he can capture and weaken a woman's feminine heart, she cannot be fully alive to her husband. After all, she can't give her beauty away if she doubts that she has it or lives in fear she will be taken advantage of when she risks offering it.

She possesses not only her beauty but her female capacity to nurture and enfold others with her essential life-giving tenderness. So, the enemy assaults her inner and outer beauty as a woman and in doing so diminishes her sense of self-worth. He corrupts how she sees herself and lies to her about her feminine glory.

The devil knows God created her with a nurturing, life-giving heart to take in and internalize their relationship. By lying and degrading her value as a woman and all that means, the devil locks her in the tower.

In the context of marriage, God has created a beautiful, life-giving ecosystem in which a woman shares her tenderness and beauty with her man and receives his strength, confidence, and masculine engagement in return. A whole marriage works this way. The emotions are good, and the sex is good. God's image is fully reflected through the union of the whole two.

But when the devil can wound a woman here, in her core female identity and value as a woman, she will feel bad about herself, agreeing with the devil's devaluing lies. Unable to feel good about herself, she struggles to feel good for her man. She can be reluctant or unable to give herself to her husband the way he needs her to, both physically and emotionally.

Unsure she is enough for him, she can be preoccupied with doubts about her beauty, looking to the world for a solution or escape. She can also become overfocused on receiving assurance from her man, which he can perceive as her being clingy and demanding.

She thinks, *Am I enough for him and beautiful enough to keep him interested in me? I want to be wanted. Not just for my body but my heart too. I need him to give himself to me, not just sexually.*

I'm lonely without his connection. I need his attention and affection and his words so I don't get overwhelmed by these negative feelings about myself. I feel reassured by His connection to me.

These are questions and needs that haunt her broken heart, springing from a fear that she won't be wanted and that she's not enough.

She wants to be wanted, and this makes her vulnerable to a man who could hurt her by not wanting, noticing, or pursuing her. Is she truly "the fairest of them all" to him? After all, look at all the competition. Neglect can reinforce awful lies in her heart about her beauty and value.

In *Love and War*, John and Staci Eldredge declare, "The scariest thing a woman ever offers is to believe she is worth pursuing, to open up her heart to the pursuit, to continue to open up her heart and offer the beauty she holds inside, all the while fearing it will not be enough."[1]

All these dynamics—insecurity, self-doubt, fear, vulnerability, and self-protection—isolate her from her man.

These are the jailors who, despite her deepest longings for connection, keep her locked in her tower, isolated and alone. God plans to heal her heart, break her agreement with the lies of the devil, and restore her feminine soul and power to be a woman fully alive.

His Life in the Tower

Satan's attack on men is like his attack on women, but to accomplish the same result—self-doubt and isolation—he targets a man's strength, confidence, and masculine engagement.

The truth is that God designed men to offer a woman the very things she needs from him: strength, leadership, confidence, security, support, and engagement. However, the devil knows if he can capture and weaken his masculine heart, he can sabotage him in his role and prevent him from being fully alive to his woman. After all, he can't give his strength away if he doubts that he has it! These qualities of his masculine design, after all, are the very things his woman needs from him—just as he needs her beauty and tenderness.

No wonder a man's identity becomes the target. No wonder Satan tries to lock a man in a tower so his woman can't get what she needs from him. The devil is the thief who comes to kill, steal, and destroy intimacy (John 10:10).

And he does it by attacking gender identity in both the masculine and feminine. A cruel blow to our sexual identities.

Can you see how the attacks are designed to lock both the man and woman in towers that prevent them from bringing what the other so deeply needs?

They are both defeated in marriage if the devil wins here and they believe the lies.

The conflict comes and the woman is left alone when the man is reluctant or unable to bring his strength to her. He fears his strength is not enough, that *he* is not enough. His struggle, like hers, is also with inadequacy but involves fear and lies about whether he has what it takes as a man—whether he's man enough. Can he really bring it; everything she needs?

Mark Gungor, in his book *Laugh Your Way to a Better Marriage*, cites a survey where 75 percent of men admitted they feel like impostors. They have fragile egos and feel criticized and disrespected easily. He then emphasizes a man's need for a woman to respect him to motivate him to change, and how debilitating her criticism and insults can be to him, embittering him.[2]

Her ego-fragile knight feels like a poser, not a ready knight in armor like she's expecting. He feels inadequate in the face of her expectations. That sword he's supposed to swing to defend her honor feels heavy. Feeling this inadequacy tempts him to withdraw from her in fear instead of taking the risk to hear her struggles, connect, and fight for her heart. Each boy needs to find the courage to become a man and raise the sword for his woman, and not retreat from her fearing his inadequacy. It is his rite of passage. He questions himself:

> *Am I enough for her and strong enough to fight for her heart and help her win the battles against her spiritual enemies? (After all, those dragons breathe fire!) What if I fail and don't have what it takes? What if I can't fix it or figure it out and it's too much for me? I feel her reaching for my strength and feel overwhelmed to meet her needs.*
>
> *I long for her body and her tenderness. I want to be wanted; I hope she doesn't reject me in my vulnerability toward her, in my need for sex, emotional connection, and validation. I need her respect and admiration; I hope she doesn't put me down. I already battle so much shame and feel weak.*

These questions and fears, coming from a fear he won't be wanted, also haunt his broken heart. Like her, he also wants to be wanted and fears she won't love his true self without him pretending and performing. He's not sure how much he can risk giving her because of how much she could hurt him by withholding or criticizing.

Again, the Eldredges reveal in *Love and War* an important truth: "The scariest thing a man ever chooses is to offer his strength without knowing how things will turn out. To take the risk of playing the man before the outcome is decided. To offer his heart of strength while fearing it will not be enough."[3]

In the garden, God came after his man, calling, "Adam, where are you?" Gen. 3:9 (I ask, *why didn't God come after Eve to find out what happened?*) and found Adam hiding among the trees of the garden, behind his fig leaf. He is afraid to offer his true self to his woman. He is tempted to abdicate his manhood, initiative, and strength and runs from his responsibilities. The serpent leaves him speechless, as he withdraws and goes silent, keeping his words and feelings from her.[4]

If this isn't an attack against our genders as men and women, why did Adam and Eve cover only their genitals with fig leaves? Because gender given by God is the image of God reflected through our maleness and femaleness. How did they "know they were naked?" (Gen. 3:11). Because the devil now had access to their hearts to shame them in their sexual identity. The devil "told them they were naked." That part of them, their sexual essence, was to be naked and unashamed before the fall (Gen. 2:25). Now, with confidence in their gender identities stolen they knew they were in trouble, so "they sewed fig leaves together" for coverings to cover their nakedness (Gen. 3:7). They were no longer naked and unashamed. They now felt shame, and afraid of who they were. Fear entered, and they felt threatened by their differences, rather than bonding over those differences.

They were no less male or female after the fall than before, but their confidence to move into their God-given roles, (identity) as a whole man and woman was fractured. Fear, shame, and confusion relating to whole sexuality entered where none had been before. A vital connection was severed between the man and the woman by the devil; hence the sword between the sexes, an enmity between them now seen working out in confusion in society through the rejection or abdication of God-given sexual gender roles (being a man or a woman.) Any rejection, or transfer of gender roles needs to be seen as a degradation of the essence of true masculinity and femininity. This includes same-sex sexual relations; this is a degrading of the image of God.

This abdicating, or weakening of the masculine role was first seen in Genesis when Adam blamed Eve and even God to avoid taking responsibility for his own silence and inaction. Instead of loving Eve and fighting for her heart, he dishonored and abandoned her as the broken masculine continues to degrade feminine beauty and vulnerability to this day. Whole masculinity will fight for and protect purity and defend femininity, in committed love, refusing to abandon the woman. It is broken men without honor who use the feminine, degrading her in doing so.

Adam demonstrates the abdication of masculine strength when he says, "The woman you gave to be with me, she gave me of the tree and I ate" (Gen. 3:14).

Adam had used Eve sexually when it was easy going in the garden, but then he abandoned her as soon as the heat was on. He backed off of love as soon as it started costing him something. He blamed Eve and God for his choice instead of taking the responsibility of owning his sin and dealing with it. As Adam's distant grandchildren, man's fear now creates in him a kind of relational cowardice, robbing him of masculine courage to engage and connect with her heart at meaningful, intimate levels. At this point, he's not man enough. Passive males should feel uneasy here.

It's important to see a man's unwillingness or inability to be present to a woman to love her properly as broken masculinity. We will show later how maturing love will choose the path to own sin and take responsibility for our part of the broken dynamics we create. Our repentance enables us to take responsibility and forsake blaming that separates us.

He can't be present in this way, and that is *why* there is conflict. He is rendered incapable or unable to engage her with strength because of the brokenness in his masculinity. When he does engage her his inadequacy often displays as defensiveness, feeling blamed, or not meeting up, so he creates distance to feel safe or puts her down to reduce the threat she represents.

This is what drives women up the wall. She reaches for his presence, participation, and engagement, and she finds a vacuum.

Where is he anyway? Why can't he show up and get involved?

So, she pressures, nags, and tries to change him, which of course deepens the disconnect as he withdraws from those painful dynamics. The reason for this narrative is to create an understanding of the cause and effect of our related dynamics that stem from our brokenness. As our identity is secured by God, the brokenness within is healed and our dynamics are transformed as we are changed inwardly by the healing grace of God.

He thinks, *I need to withhold my strength, engagement, partici-pation, and leadership from her to be safe; I can't let my guard down, or I might be exposed as the impostor I am. My inability to come through will prove my worst fear, that I don't have what it takes to be the man she needs.*

Because of this fear, the man feels compelled to withhold his strength from his woman, as he feels unsure, tentative, and inadequate. He's not sure he's enough. Of course, if he withholds, this sends her to the tower as she believes his fail-ure to pursue her only confirms her feelings of inadequacy and low self-worth. This cements a pursue-retreat cycle that enforces loneliness and frustration, while connection seems a mirage.

When rejected by her, or when she withholds intimacy (sex) from him, he may believe, *She doesn't want me emotionally or sexually. She just wants my strength and performance. I don't feel like I'm enough for what she needs from me. I feel used and unappre-ciated, and she still wants more from me.*

This is what our beleaguered prince believes, leaving him barred in his tower, agreeing with lies, and telling himself every day, *I'm not enough.* Like young Simba in *The Lion King*, he can't shake the lies and shame of the past and is afraid to take the kingdom that belongs to him. The one with his name on it that waits for him to return and claim. It seems out of reach to him, but in time he may grow into the man he needs to become to take his rightful place in *his* kingdom.

Every man has a kingdom he's called to take, to move into his destiny as a man. He needs empowerment to claim his mas-culine strength to return and fight the battles, slay his dragons, and let God break the curse. (Piece of cake.) God plans to heal his heart with the woman, affirm his manhood, and restore his masculine identity. This plan includes the lovers seeking God for strategy together to defeat the enemy who has wounded their souls and their identities.

Notice the struggle is the same for the man and the woman: inadequacy, lacking the courage to offer *themselves,* both struggling because of the lies to believe they are enough.

What Men and Women Long For—Reassurance

Like Eve, Adam also wants to be wanted and needs reassurance that he's enough and has what it takes for his woman. Unlike Eve, he doesn't find his reassurance through romance, at least not in the same way she does. I'm not giving anything away by saying he finds his reassurance mostly through sex. Who knew?

Willard Harley reveals in *His Needs, Her Needs* that sexual fulfillment is the number one thing he can't do without.[5] Every woman knows this, and it's the key to getting her tower unlocked as well, although she may have a hard time believing it's this simple.

Men need sex because it meets their number one need: reassurance that they're loved, desired, and have value. Affection and romance are her love language; sexual fulfillment is his. We'll explore sexual differences between men and women more in the "Celebrate the Gift of Sexuality" chapter, but here are a couple of differences in the context of this discussion.

Most know that women and men are wired differently when it comes to sexual motivation. Research shows that women usually need an emotional connection to desire sex with their husbands, whereas most men can enjoy sex with their wives even if they feel disconnected emotionally. They don't need as much emotional ramping up or preparation beforehand. (I don't know how else to say it.)

Willard Harley explains in *His Needs Her Needs* that women who are emotionally withdrawn from their husbands are often unwilling to have sex with him. (When he neglects her, she withdraws.) If she doesn't feel emotionally close to him, she won't want to make love to him. That's why affection is the environment that makes the event of sex attractive to most women.[6] For more details and support, *His Needs, Her Needs* is an excellent practical resource.

Breaking the Spell

A man's love, affection, and value he bestows on his woman give her the courage she needs to unveil her beauty to him. She wants to give herself to him because she feels his love and his care for her heart. A woman who feels cherished by her husband won't face the struggles to give herself to him that an unloved woman will have. I understand how pain, degradation, and neglect can shut a heart down and send someone to the tower. There is hope to follow the Good Shepherd out into freedom and connection.

Can you see that the towers are gender specific, but the core attacks are the same? The lie is the same: *You are not enough.*

For her, the lie is *You are not woman enough* in things connected to beauty and womanhood. This attacks her self-esteem and worth, and she feels vulnerable. Without his sensitivity, love, and affirmation, she can feel taken advantage of.

For him, the lie is *You are not man enough* in things connected to manhood and masculine strength. This attacks his confidence as a man, and inadequacy tempts him to back off his role as warrior-provider-lover and, as pursuer of her heart. If he gives into the pressure of the lies, he can withhold the strength she needs to thrive. It's easier for him to perform than risk vulnerability and love tenderly. (It's interesting to note that women desire the feminine qualities that the true masculine also possesses.) A man without these nurturing skills fails the command to love his wife as Christ loved the church by giving his life, and to nourish, cherish, and protect her (Eph. 5:25–29).

Lies targeting beauty and strength damage our identities as men and women. These lies fuel a diabolical attack on these identities in specific ways that sabotage our ability to come through for each other in the ways we need and desire.

Healing from these lies — which is the inevitable quest on which we all must embark — brings us into wholeness and empowers us to express our unique glory as men and women.

Empathy can flow from us to the opposite sex when we understand their struggle and do what we can to alleviate their pain and reassure them they are loved and desired and more than enough. (That's why we married them.)

CHAPTER THREE
The Curse of Stolen Identity

The fallen self cannot know itself. We do not know who we are and will search for an identity in someone or something other than God until we find ourselves in Him.

—Leanne Payne

God created us with a divine soul only he can satisfy and fill. You know that aching longing and desire we feel for "something more"? He put that desire in our souls so that he could satisfy it. Our souls find rest in him when we learn to encounter him in our emptiness and loneliness.

When we wonder why life can leave us feeling empty, even in marriage, God has the answer: *He* is the one who "satisfies the longing soul, and fills the hungry soul with goodness" (Ps. 107:9).

Our dilemma and snare is that we try to fill that void with all sorts of things. We try to fill the emptiness ourselves, and it gets us into trouble looking for purpose, life, and love in the wrong places. We look to things like jobs, addictions, power, lovers, and more to tell us who we are and fill the void inside. All of these are examples of stolen identity—all these can become idols of worship that imprison rather than satisfy us.

God invites us to begin our search for identity, love, purpose, and healing by looking to him—and promises that if we start there, good things in our marriage will follow (Matt. 6:33). He wants to recover and secure our genuine identities and heal our wounded hearts with his love. He calls for us and romances our hearts so we will love him with all our heart and strength. This is the invitation to the inward journey.

We can't give ourselves away to another if we are lost and don't know who we are. It's our search for our stolen identities that keeps us from giving our whole selves to each other in marriage. It's because of what we've lost that we end up in the two towers. Now we're married to someone and we're trying to find it—that completeness and fulfillment—but we just aren't sure what it is. Have you ever thought or felt:

- *I thought marriage would be this affirming, connected, validating place. Now I feel unsure.*
- *I thought I would never feel alone again when I married, but now I feel invisible. What happened?*
- *Why can't they just accept me for who I am? Why do I feel this performance pressure to change or be someone else?*

In our quest for a better marriage, God understands our desire to turn to our spouses for our identity, purpose, and healing. After all, we married them and they're right next to us to give us everything we could need. He also knows that looking to our lovers for these things will leave us as empty and frustrated as when we began.

Let God Use Your Marriage to Reveal Who You Are and Who You Long to Be

When our marriage starts polarizing, we begin to face our true selves and the masks we use to hide behind. This doesn't sound like fun and it isn't! This is where the image of who we thought we married starts fading, then evaporates. This is hard for us because we fell in love with that image. When that goes away — anxiety elevates as we can think we've fallen out of love or made a mistake and married the wrong person.

These are anxious times when our idealized images and expectations are exposed along with our weaknesses and operating systems. We didn't know anything about those, or even aware they existed. This is our invitation to transformation, but we don't know it yet. Our insecure, scared selves can feel they can't take anymore as they are reflected in the mirrors of our spouses. (And they're sleeping in the same bed with us. They see everything!)

It's hard to believe that finding our stolen identity could have anything to do with the one we married — especially if we thought they were the ones who were to restore it to us. It's scarier still to think God had it planned and even picked the one he would use to expose us to our weaknesses and hiding places. Many are unaware of how God is working at this time and focus only on their spouse, and how they are causing them pain and resisting them.

How did our lover turn into our pain-giver? How could this be love?

The classic power struggle begins in the couple as they start controlling and resisting instead of cooperating and inviting God in. It helps to say here that we don't have experience inviting God into this process that feels so foreign and painful. We thought marriage would solve our problems and instead, it seems to have created more, and we didn't anticipate any of this.

God understands how much this hurts when what we expect and need isn't coming to us the way we thought it would or should. He draws near to comfort us in our pain and disappointment as we see our unfulfilled expectations and dreams die. We may think, *I thought I was going to get so much more out of this than how it's turning out.*

This reflection and exposure is normal and for our freedom, not our peril. When we feel threatened, it's natural to retreat and avoid pain if possible. God gives us the grace, courage, and new commitment to change what we've always done to survive — run and hide.

Our covenant in marriage helps us stand and be honest about ourselves and how we feel with our partners as we see our true state and our insufficiencies. Our faith grows as we encounter God and gain an understanding of his process. Only then, with new courage, can we acknowledge our patterns and let him transform them. This is the positive, grace-filled doorway into authentic relating that leads us into the sustaining intimacy we long for.

God is approaching us through our spouse to reveal our true selves to us. We aren't accustomed to such intimacy. We want *them* to be the problem, not reflect our brokenness to us!

I was shocked when I married Linda and saw how much of my relating was being done underground. My manipulative ways were exposed and I was humbled by my neediness, wounds, and unaffirmed areas in my heart. God was coaxing me out of denial as he exposed my self-centered world and its motives. I had to admit I was a wreck.

I asked God, *Really? That's what I'm doing? I'm projecting this onto her. What can I do?*

Go tell her what I just showed you, see what she says, and take it from there. I'll help you.

This began establishing the healing environment in our marriage we still enjoy today, as we take the risks of vulnerability and honesty.

God the Father wants to restore identity to our true *selves*. (He can't heal masks.) He calls us out of hiding for this to happen. He wants us to get real with him. The little boy is becoming a man, and the little girl a woman, but they must find themselves along the way. Don't run and hide from him when he calls for you.

This is where God's power encounters our personality. This is when spiritual change happens as he joins with the true "us." This is when we drop our fig leaves and get real.

Let God Meet the Needs Your Marriage Can't Meet

One morning these words came into my head as I awoke: *A spouse can keep you company, but only God can tell you who you are.*

This tells me God gave Eve to Adam because he didn't want him to be lonely, not for Eve to replace God. Adam needs the woman. God himself said, "It's not good for the man to be alone. I will make him a helper comparable to him" (Gen. 2:18 NIV).

If God intended to solely meet *all* our needs, he wouldn't have created Eve for Adam and gifted us with marriage to ease our aloneness. He never said our spouse would take our inner loneliness and emptiness away. He didn't give Eve to Adam so she would become his goddess with her surreal beauty, replacing God in his life. Nor did he give Adam to Eve so he could be her masculine god, as ripped as he might be, replacing God's place on the throne of her heart.

Yet we do this, make them our gods, when we expect them to meet the critical needs only God can.

Author Alex Avila says, "Sometimes we can place unfair pressure on our partner to meet all our needs. When it comes to our core needs, however, it's important to distinguish which ones our partner is designed and capable to meet, and which needs we must rely on God and ourselves to meet. Our purpose for living comes from God, not people."[1]

Our spouses can help, but they can't do it all. All the sex or intimate connection we can get can't be what drives our purpose for living. Looking there can only lead to addiction.

The woman can't tell the man who he is and give him an identity, and he can't provide hers. It's not humanly possible to extract the spiritual quality of identity from flesh and blood. You can't get your identity from someone else, and things go sideways when you try.

What we need to secure our identity comes from a spiritual source, namely God, who knows what we need. It can't come from the *creature*; only the *Creator* can restore the broken image of the one he made.

The Million-Dollar Question

How then do we know what our spouse can give us and what we need to go to God for? Sure, we're all familiar with fairy-tale fantasies where people say of their beloved, "They will complete me." But can they?

God designed marriage and the mutually submitted model it contains for this unique purpose: to meet our human needs. No one else on earth can meet your need for affection, sex, or emotional connection like your spouse. This is the companionship piece.

Marriage gives both partners a powerful opportunity to validate, meet needs, love, and affirm at heart levels unavailable in relationships outside marriage. Think of it this way: there are parts of your wounded, battered heart that are waiting to be healed, and God will use you both, as loving spouses, to facilitate that healing in each other.

As we'll see in future chapters, acceptance, honor, respect, and validation are all powerful, healing forces when we learn to apply them. This is what I mean when I say we can love each other to life, by functioning as husband and wife as God intended.

Being loved to life,

- we learn, in the fear of God, to enter the holy of holies of each other's hearts as we develop security and acceptance in marriage;
- we speak the truth in love to each other and provide a safe environment to resolve differences, grow, love, and explore;
- we learn to connect heart to heart through honoring and validating in ways we've never experienced.

There's nothing I know on the human level as powerful and healing as these.

When we are giving ourselves to our spouses in unconditional love, we *are* loving them to life, but we are not the *source* of life, nor are we to be worshipped as such. Our spouses can keep us company, but they just won't, and can't fill the emptiness only God can fill.

God is our source, and only he can break the spell over us and bring the transformation we need to get out of our towers. "True love's kiss" can't do it. No man or woman can do it. Only Jesus, the hero of our stories, can "complete" and heal our hearts, giving us meaning, significance, and purpose. We're called to love God with all our hearts and have no other gods before him (Ex. 20:3; Mark 12:30). Our true identity is found in him.

How Do I Know When I'm Overreaching?

If the princess or prince reaches for a spouse to be their god or goddess, they will expect from them a kind of love no human can give. I think we all do it at first, in our immature love. We reach for the stars, fly too close to the sun, and our wings melt.

Men tend to have simpler fairy-tale thinking about their wives' roles in serving them, specifically being sexually available, and hopefully feeding them, while women's fairy-tale thinking tends more toward expectations about their emotional needs being met through ongoing connection and romantic pursuit.

Women are built generally with a deeper capacity (and desire) to internalize emotions and relationships than men are. God made them beautiful in this regard on purpose. They generally value going deeper in the relationship than the man, not that he doesn't want to; he just has different wiring and doesn't feel the need to go deeper into the emotional realms she enjoys.

Ladies hope to fill this hunger for deeper relating and connection through a more involved relationship with their husbands. They desire and need intimate involvement with the heart and feelings of their busy man. She doesn't want to be left out – she wants to be included and connected to his life. This makes her vulnerable to neglect. Him being unavailable to her and shutting her out of his life sends her to the tower.

These unmet needs can create a state of disappointment and a strong desire for things to be different. Indeed, our expectations can chain us to a disappointed state in life if we don't work to adjust them to the reality of the love we are experiencing. Anxiety is a symptom of this false belief operating – the belief that our spouses are the means to our fulfillment.

At these times, we must go to God and our partner to process our needs and expectations in the relationship. This takes vulnerability and a willingness to risk honesty. We will connect if we are courageous here.

Will I Trust God and love? Or Take Over and Manipulate?

Words begin to fail when talking about identity, idolatry, and meeting core needs. Living by the law of love provides simplicity and answers we can find no other way. The Quest we're on is one of mutual love and spiritual growth. The question above says it all. Love will tell the truth and openly process and negotiate dynamics, choices, and actions. When we move out of love, we move into the realm of hidden manipulation, undisclosed relating, and pressure tactics. Most of us do this in immature love.

I will overreach when I fixate on my spouse to get more from them than I'm getting. When we stop trusting God to meet our needs, we stop loving and move into compulsion. This means we feel compelled to start controlling and taking things into our own hands. We see that our partner isn't coming through for us so we decide we will try to *make them come through*. This is where it gets bad.

When we take over with clenched fists, we feel frustrated and anxious and choke out freedom and spontaneity of the marriage. These emotions reveal the telltale symptoms that something is amiss in our hearts. We lose the fruit of love, joy, and peace when we move into takeover mode. We regain that fruit through repentance, by opening our hands again and talking to our spouse instead of manipulating them.

We overreach to our spouses for what we need, expecting it, thinking they possess it. We try to figure out a way to extract it from them. Both men and women can do this as need and longing are common to both. Apart from yielding to God and trusting him, we *will* take over, convinced our spouses have the cure for our empty hearts and are withholding it.

There's no one-step answer to the freedom journey. It comes as we work through each struggle and conflict that arises. Our freedom comes when we can see what we're doing, modify our expectations, and adjust to reality. This is the path to committed love.

We will know when our control is not working. We will feel frustrated and discouraged that our efforts are failing. With an empty bucket, we can take our focus off our spouses and put them back on Jesus. Returning to God, repenting, and giving him the rightful place in our hearts is how we regain our freedom (Zech 1:3; Hos. 6:1). We do this as often as we need to, which is when we hit the wall and face our frustration. This is the language of the heart involving yielding to the spirit of God in our pain, and sometimes loneliness, as we look to him for what only he can give.

Our problems can stem from our spouses, but more often they stem from ourselves and our relationship with God. These are heart issues of faith and idolatry. Our inability to trust God and seek him as the source of our core needs is the problem.

Finding Freedom

To be free, we must come out of agreement with the idolatrous belief that says if I can just get them to cooperate with me, I can get what I need from them to fill me.

In essence, I must forsake my idol of getting my needs met on my terms and return to the one who can fill me. It's easier said than done to break down false beliefs, especially if they've been ingrained into our thinking, but we *can* overcome them if we identify them. There is power in identifying our behavioral drivers and dismantling them. We can choose how we are going to act and who we are going to be.

When I realize I am overreaching, I return to God and offer my heart and struggles anew. I gain the wisdom I need to realign with him—by putting Him back in his rightful place. I can then choose to trust him for my needs and stop manipulating my partner for what I must have. I am never alone or empty in that place, and he fills me with his presence, which is more fulfilling than whatever else I'm going after. He consumes my loneliness and the ache I feel in my heart. He truly turns my desert into a garden.

God wants to show us a way of meeting our needs and still allowing our partners to be who they are.

This is the way of faith, to engage our lovers without controlling them. We can't control them to meet our needs. We must cut the cord we have put on them that says, *You're the key to my happiness; make me happy.*

Rather, we say to God, "Father, I give my spouse to you and release them to you. Come and give me what my heart needs right now. I wait for You. Only You can give me what I need. I surrender."

We will find, in learning to love, that meeting each other's needs is conditional and must be negotiated as we unpack and modify our expectations. Through honest relating and forsaking manipulation, we can discover the truth in our dynamics and invite our partners to negotiate for what they can do to meet our needs. We respect what they can give, trusting God with the rest. We risk vulnerability with them about our disappointment and honestly talk it through.

He wants our hearts free to love, and they can't love when we create idols that enslave us. He doesn't want us attached and addicted and left alone. Letting go is the key to taking our focus off our spouse and looking to Jesus.

Our confusion leaves when we go to him in surrender and find he's waiting there for us. At times, he's the one who frustrates our efforts to find "completion" through our spouses. He's a jealous God and won't allow idolatry for our good. The truth that frees us from the idolatry trap is this: no amount of connection to our spouse, whether it's trying to connect through romance or sex, will fill our longing hearts. Knowing this, we can choose to take the pressure off our spouse and our marriage and look to God for this essential connection, and he will fill the needs of our deep hearts.

I have always found relief when he shows me I'm over-reaching to my spouse for something I need. I become aware that my dynamics are self-serving, and I can see the futility of my efforts. He shows me how I'm pushing and striving and why. I surrender and ask him to show me the better way of humility and love. I then wait in faith for him to provide what I need, whether from him or my loving spouse who willingly gives me what she can.

CHAPTER FOUR

Invite the Hero of
Your Story into Your Quest

For the Son of Man has come to
seek and to save that which was lost.

—Luke 19:10

This chapter is about inviting Jesus, the hero of our stories into our marriages—and the process involved in growing us into mature lovers. Only he can bring the hope, wisdom, and grace we need to thrive— connected and empowered as we pursue our dream of oneness.

Did you know that we were never meant to rescue ourselves, our spouses, and our marriages by ourselves?

The truth is that there is a Hero who longs to help us in the transformative process of becoming one in marriage.

Jesus declared why he came when he stood up in the temple in Jerusalem and read from the scroll of Isaiah, "He has sent Me to heal the brokenhearted, to proclaim liberty to the captives, and the opening of the prison to those who are bound" (Isa. 61:1).

God uses our marriages like nothing else in the process of transforming us into his image.

Jesus is asking us to welcome him into our quest and allow him to reveal and heal our wounded hearts. Only our Hero Prince of Peace can break the spell over our hearts.

To do this means we encounter him in the five priceless gifts that he is offering us:

1. The Transformative Gift of Salvation
2. The Transformative Gift of Spiritual Growth
3. The Transformative Gift of Redemptive Conflict
4. The Transformative Gift of a Renewed Mind
5. The Transformative Gift of the Cross

1. The Transformative Gift of Salvation

Everything good we experience in life, love, and marriage comes from the gift the Father sent to us when he sent Jesus.

- Jesus came to Earth as a man to seek and save our lost hearts.

  He came for us individually, personally, and intimately. Our yes to Jesus invites him into our hearts to give us new life and walk with us out of darkness into light.

- He broke the spells of sin and curses over our lives and calls us to follow Him (Gal. 3:13–14).

  Our walk with Him empowers us to be free from any prison in spiritual life that would hold us. The light of his truth and love frees us.

- Jesus redeemed us and provided forgiveness from sin by dying on the cross (Heb. 12:2).

  "In Him we have redemption through His blood, the forgiveness of sins, according to the riches of His grace" (Eph. 1:7).

All the gifts we will see next are wrapped up in his gift of salvation, and we will find that he is at the center of our quest at every step. When we receive the gift of salvation, we enter into a faith relationship with Jesus. He becomes the hero of our story who makes all deliverance and freedom possible. He has promised to give us his Holy Spirit and to never leave us alone.

2. The Transformative Gift of Spiritual Growth

God's plan during our feelings of loss, pain, and confusion in the disillusionment stage is to start transforming us into mature lovers. We can't mature on "easy love," so he takes us off the bottle and starts us on solid food to grow us into committed love.

First Corinthians 13 is called the love chapter in the Bible. In it, Paul writes, "When I was a child, I spoke as a child, I understood as a child, I thought as a child; but when I became a man, I put away childish things" (1 Cor. 13:11).

Babies learn early that the louder they cry, the faster help comes. They aren't concerned with the interruption or inconvenience they are causing. Adults, we hope, move out of this crybaby pattern to more advanced forms of relating, like honest, patient communication about needs and desires.

Marriage pushes our "baby" buttons without us even thinking about it. Intentional choices are needed to grow up and out of our immature attitudes and approaches to life. Here's what some of these choices look like:

Baby Love	Adult Love
Impatient emotions	Long-suffering emotions
Demands instant gratification	Accepts delayed gratification
Selfish, self-focused	Giving, others-oriented
Can't sacrifice	Can say no to self
Demands own way	Yields to others' desires
Outbursts of anger	Self-controlled
Insecure, defensive	Secure, open
Fearful, unable to trust	Fearless, risks trusting
Proud, self-important	Humble, not easily offended
Stubborn, unyielding	Flexible, tender
Ungrounded, unstable	Rooted, grounded
Me first	You first
Unforgiving, punishing	Forgiving, gracious
No empathy to see others' pain	Empathetic, compassionate
Rebels at disappointment	Processes disappointment with God
Controlling	Frees others

It's normal to resist this process of growth because our flesh has grown used to baby love. If we don't get our way, we're quick to react and resist. When it comes to meeting needs, we care more about ours than theirs. When honoring differences, we hate that they are different and resist them. When it comes to change — instead of yielding — we think our spouses should conform to our desires, and resist when they won't cooperate.

These new dynamics aren't fun. We want things to be easy and simple like before. It's normal to feel discouraged and want to check out on many levels.

But this is the beginning of learning to die to self as we realize the cost of loving deeply from the heart. And if we resist taking the challenge, we'll stay in an immature love state driven by selfishness that pushes us down joyless paths of manipulation, control, and relational bondage.

Polarization is God's gift to us to free us from these chains and to grow us into mature lovers so our marriage can not only survive but thrive. Without this push to grow, we would remain self-focused babies, unable to love and sacrifice.

Realizing marriage isn't all we expected is painful.

It's even more discouraging as we realize, "It is *me* God wants to change."

Yet, if we're honest with ourselves, we just might admit that, deep down, we want this. We don't *really* want to be selfish, we just haven't learned a better way yet, and there's a part of us that longs to do better, be better, as we are transformed into the mature lovers God created us to be.

To make the most of this precious gift, you must be willing to do three things:

Grow spiritually, own your stuff, and meet the needs of your spouse.

Grow Spiritually

Spiritual growth is the pathway to committed love that draws us beyond eros and into true covenant. This means bailing out on the marriage as an option is taken off the table. We will see this ahead in the *Securing the Castle* chapter. Spiritual growth is born out of our commitment to honor God no matter the cost. A marriage grows as two individuals grow spiritually. Whatever it takes, we determine that we are going to ride this out.

We can only enjoy mutuality as we grow out of ourselves in love to honor and care for another. Growth in love is spiritual growth. This is the putting away of our childish things. We come to a place where we value *us* more than *me*. The quest for spiritual growth is ongoing as we honor God and our covenant to him and one another. We demonstrate this growth as we learn to practice these things and grow out of that baby love into the God kind of love that reflects his kingdom.

Own Your Stuff

We grow together spiritually as we learn to take responsibility for, and "own," our sins and brokenness before God and our spouse. We repent of them when God exposes them to us.

In the garden, when God asked Adam if he had eaten fruit from the forbidden tree, we remember that he blamed Eve, and Eve blamed the devil. A marriage can't grow unless both partners commit to owning their stuff and forsake the blame game.

When there is something in me—a sinful attitude, pattern, or behavior—causing pain and conflict in our marriage, I choose to own my stuff. I could be dishonoring or degrading to my wife by giving her the silent treatment or using sarcasm. It might be something about my personality that offends her — insensitivity and hurtful words. Whatever it is, owning it means that I see it, confess it, and bring it into the light to be dealt with.

It is "dealt with" when

- I don't deny my behavior, blame my spouse, make her responsible for my behavior, or play other childish games.
- I release the offending behavior with humility and love.
- I repent and ask God to transform me, deepen my ability to love, and help me respond differently in the future.

My experience has been that owning my part always draws God's power and grace into our relationship and changes (transforms) the dynamics. Truth and honesty always carry power in enabling forgiveness from God and our spouse. Yielding and repentance invite Him in.

It takes courage to embrace the truth about our broken patterns of relating. We need courage because we know we are weak and reactive, still carry shame, and need grace to face our insufficiency and wounds to "own" them.

Taking responsibility means obedience — I own up to my part of what's making us hurt and act on it by being willing to see who I am — without denying or blaming:

Yes, I see what I'm doing, and now I see why. Lord, help me grow and heal so I don't have to use this broken pattern to get what I want.

When I own my stuff, it attracts the power of the Holy Spirit to change me. He joins me in my agreement with him about myself, empowering change and growth. It's important to see that he is authorizing this; it's not the devil or your stubborn spouse.

This courage is given by Jesus, the hero of our stories when we invite him into the process. We invite him in when we say yes to him, the one authorizing the very thing we are experiencing. This takes faith. As soon as you step out, he meets you.

Meet the Needs of Your Spouse

We shared in chapter 2, *Life in Separate Towers*, how men and women have the same fundamental needs and want the same things—which are love, validation, and reassurance. When they don't get these things, both men and women experience the same painful emotions, feeling unloved, lonely, and depressed. We've described these emotions as life in the tower.

The challenge for us is found in our tendency to seek fulfillment of our fundamental needs in opposite ways. What one feels they can't live without, the other could take or leave, and vice versa. Remember, he's wired more for sex, and she's wired more for relational intimacy and emotional connection.

When I make choices that honor my wife and make her happy, even if it's not what I want most, or at all, I choose to honor her desires over myself. I will learn about her heart, desires, and needs, and how I can meet her there by showing attention and interest in her. I must grow spiritually to be able to do this. I tell her, "I want to know about your heart, how you feel, what you need and want, and how I can care about those things."

You can almost hear the hinges of the tower door swinging open as she steps out to respond to healing love. In response, she may do the same thing for me.

The good news is that the potential for intimacy this creates is immeasurable. Our differences are the doorway, not a wall. We just need to find the key.

We grow in wisdom, understanding, and empathy as we explore what our partner needs and how we can meet them there with our commitment to love. This is the "quest," the exciting process of "loving each other to life."

3. The Transformative Gift of Redemptive Conflict

The subject of conflict has received a bad rap. Here are a few of the lies we believe about it:

- Conflict is bad so we should avoid any conversations that upset us.
- Conflict is ungodly, so Christians with good marriages don't fight.
- Conflict is from the devil.
- If we fight, it means we have marriage problems.
- If we are in God's will, there will be no conflict.
- God's presence in our marriages means we won't fight.

It figures the devil would vilify the very process God uses to grow and connect us — The School of Conflict. If the devil can convince us conflict is ungodly or evil, he has defeated us before we've even started. Much of our spiritual life involves allowing God to grow us through conflicts and trials; how much more in marriage? (see James 1:2-4; Rom. 12:12; Eph. 4:15, 25).

Here are some truths about conflict that can help us: Conflict is God's vehicle of transformation in marriage when yielded to him. Simply stated — if we avoided disagreeing over differences — our true selves wouldn't be exposed, and we would keep hiding behind our masks and the games we play. The conflict reveals who we are, what we are doing, and the way through. This is a faith-building insight! God is actually behind our conflict and very much a part of it.

In essence, our conflicts are God's timeline and strategy for us to work on the next broken pattern — we are fighting *because* brokenness is there. The fight reveals our issues, so we can see them and address them — in doing so, our needs and fears come to light to be met.

This is redemptive conflict — this is spiritual growth. Our conflicts reveal in us what God wants to work on as we unpack it. It's in the process of this unpacking — using learned skills while engaged in the conflict— that we connect and go deeper together.

Conflict is our growth school if we enroll in the classes. I didn't know any of this when I married Linda. I had read some books and figured I was on my way. I had no idea, and God sent me to school where I learned this stuff through the process. Our conflicts can teach us how to fight fairly, communicate with integrity, honor feelings, and validate differences.

In *The Best of A.W. Tozer*, there is an article titled "Miracles Follow the Plow." Here he describes what applies to every marriage.

He quotes Hosea 10:12: Sow for yourselves righteousness; reap in mercy; break up your fallow ground, for it is time to seek the LORD, till He comes and rains righteousness on you.

He then describes two kinds of ground:

- The fallow field is content but unproductive.
- The cultivated field, on the other hand, is productive because it has experienced "the shock of the plow and the agitation of the harrow . . . has felt the travail of change; it has been upset, turned over, bruised and broken, but its rewards come hard upon its labors."[1]

Resolving conflict together is nothing less than surrendering to the "plow of God" in our marriage. This process —though it feels severe—makes our marriage productive for bearing life and the good fruit of love, honor, and connection.

This is the quest; if you disqualify conflict, no one is freed from their tower, and mutual submission won't be enjoyed. We boldly enter into conflict to resolve issues of power and control, unmet needs, undefined roles, responsibility, and the many issues marriage involves.

Understanding redemptive conflict empowers us not to fear it but rather to engage it with courage and purpose— inviting our hero into it.

4. The Transformative Gift of a Renewed Mind

The phrase "transformed by the renewing of your mind" comes from Romans 12:2: "And do not be conformed to this world, but be transformed by the renewing of your mind, that you may prove what is that good and acceptable and perfect will of God."

When we renew our minds with God's Word, our worldly beliefs and value systems are shifted to kingdom ones. We no longer live as cookie-cutter worldly, self-seeking individuals, but we are changed by the power of a transformed mind.

Here's how our minds are renewed:

> We replace the lies and distortions of the devil with the powerful truth of God's Word. This breaks strongholds, demolishes lies, and changes how we live.

> We learn new patterns of thinking and embrace new beliefs that change how we relate to each other. Our core values are overhauled to imitate the kingdom of God.

> We learn the rules of an "upside-down" kingdom of God and operate under these new rules. We serve others instead of using them; we become others-focused rather than self-serving. We seek humility instead of grasping to be the best or first.

5. The Transformative Gift of the Cross

Jesus says, "Follow Me."

Where do we follow him? To the cross—there, after we choose to follow him, we give up our way for his way.

"Then Jesus said to His disciples, 'If anyone desires to come after Me, let him deny himself, and take up his cross, and follow Me" (Matt. 16:24). "And whoever does not bear his cross and come after Me cannot be My disciple" (Luke 14:27).

Only through the cross can we be set free from the tyranny of our compulsion to control everything and others while resisting the growth we need in our own lives. There is no change apart from the transforming power of the cross of Jesus Christ. Here are two verses that bring this home for me:

> For the message of the cross is foolishness to those who are perishing, but to us who are being saved, it is the power of God. (1 Cor. 1:18)

> Knowing this, that our old man is crucified with Him, that the body of sin might be done away with, that we should no longer be slaves of sin. (Rom. 6:6)

When we think of the cross of Jesus, we think of it as something Jesus died on to save us. We think of it as our key to heaven (which it is) and all that waits for us there. When Jesus said, "It is finished," as he died, he was talking about the price he was paying for our full redemption. It was finished for him but not for us.

Our work is just beginning. That's why we must deny ourselves and take up our cross, so we can be like him. He plans to change us into his image. For this to happen, our "self" image—the false self we live for—must be denied; it must die and be resurrected in the newness of life.

"But we all, with unveiled faces, beholding as in a mirror the glory of the Lord, are being transformed into the same image from glory to glory, just as by the Spirit of the Lord" (2 Cor. 3:18). I see this as the mission statement for life, with all else following. To be like Jesus.

I think of denying self as freedom from the tyranny of the self-life, rather than something I have to give up. All I'm giving up is futility, compulsion, and frustration. Living for self is torment and an empty search for satisfaction that doesn't exist outside of Christ. It keeps us from love because it is self-centered and self-serving.

Everything in our self-life keeps us from pursuing love and serving kingdom values. It's proud, contentious, and rebellious. That's why the cross is imperative; the self must be denied, and it must die, daily, on a cross.

A.W. Tozer says in his essay "The Cross Is a Radical Thing,"

- If we are wise, we will do what Jesus did: endure the cross and despise its shame for the joy that is set before us. To do this is to submit the whole pattern of our lives to be destroyed and built again in the power of an endless life. . . .
- It [the cross] will defeat us and bring our selfish lives to an end. Only then can we rise in newness of life to establish a pattern of living wholly new and free and full of good works.[2]

This new pattern of living is the hope of the gospel message and our hope for a "happily ever after" marriage. Our willingness to bear our cross *is our quest*, and no more so than in our marriages where we are called to die to many things so we can love our spouses well.

What does it mean to take up our cross? Once again, I quote from Mr. Tozer:

> What He does intend is that each of us should count himself dead indeed with Christ, and then accept willingly whatever of self-denial, repentance, humility, and humble sacrifice that may be found in obedient daily living. That is his cross, and it is the only one the Lord has invited him to bear.[3]

Taking up our cross in marriage and denying ourselves means choosing to submit to the process of becoming one. But we can't do this without the power of the cross. We are too stubborn and proud and cannot submit to another at the level a good marriage requires without taking up our crosses. Only the Holy Spirit can enable us to find those levels of intimacy through holy submission.

It's not as scary as it sounds.

This is transformation: allowing the power of the cross to defeat all that keeps us from love, releasing that same love from the heart of the Father into us. This brings the supernatural power of God to bear on our marriage union, reflecting his glory to the fullest. It's for real.

I want to balance this out with one more quote from A.W. Tozer:

> "But we must not get the impression that the Christian life is one continuous conflict, one un-

broken, irritating struggle against the world, the flesh, and the devil. A thousand times no.

The heart that learns to die with Christ soon knows the blessed experience of rising with Him, and all the world's persecutions cannot still the high note of holy joy that springs up in the soul that has become the dwelling place of the Holy Spirit."[4]

Chapter Five

Secure the Castle

The foundational component of an excellent marriage is a truly secure environment — one that is secure physically, intellectually, spiritually, and emotionally.

— Gary Smalley

To secure something means to make it safe. When we secure our castles, we make them a safe place, a defensible fortress. You've heard the military saying "Secure the perimeter." We install security systems in our vehicles, homes, and places of business to protect our investments and our property.

When you marry someone, you need to secure your relationship. You install a "relational security system" together that makes things safe and secure on many levels. There are things now that belong to you and your partner *exclusively*, namely each other. Trust and safety are developed in your intimate relationship together. You believe in each other and become vulnerable.

There are specific things we can do as married couples to "secure our perimeters." Castles of old had moats around them, often stocked with alligators to discourage unwelcome visitors. We must be vigilant, not passive when it comes to security.

On a recent cruise, at one of the ports, we took a walk and found an old castle protected by large rusty cannons high on the shoreline bluffs. We marveled at the enduring big guns designed to defend against pirates who could otherwise sail in to rob and plunder unless blown out of the water. Looking into the wind over the sea, you could imagine the sails of the approaching ships, hear the shouts and the blast of the cannons, and smell the gunpowder.

Our marriage is our castle and needs security. We simply won't have the resources to improve our marriages if we feel we are under constant threat. We're all familiar with the factors that can threaten our marriage; Temptation. Work. Stress. Finances. Health. Family.

We will also be blocked from connecting in our marriages if we feel constant threats from *within*. If our castles aren't safe and secure, we may start using those big cannons to fire on each other. We may try to blow their tower down, rather than coax our lover out of them. We all know how easy that can be before we've learned to fight fair.

It's easier to use power to remove the threat another represents than to use diplomacy to connect. Gunpowder and blowing things up are not the best solution or the highest road when dealing with another heart. In our baby love, we will be tempted to light the fuse and bully, using destructive power or invalidation to get our way. These are dynamics God wants to expose and heal, or we will continue to block growth and intimacy with these destructive dynamics. It's hard to become one with a bully or a degrader whether male or female.

We want to make our marriage a safe place where we're not attacking or abandoning one another, walking on eggshells, or hiding our feelings. Walking on eggshells means you are not emotionally safe with your partner. You aren't free to discuss whatever needs discussing without being degraded in the conversation.

We degrade by invalidating or ridiculing another when they open their heart. Statements like "You shouldn't feel that way, that's stupid. You're so emotional. You can't live by your feelings all the time." Or any other comment that shuts your heart down. Comments like these send the relational message that you can't be the real you or you will be put down. You are not accepted. Without boundaries, we let others define who we are by their broken dynamics and remain isolated in our towers because it's unsafe.

Sarcasm also dishonors, as do impatience and angry outbursts. (Instead, love is patient and kind.) The castle is secured when we learn to talk and act in loving, patient, and honoring ways.

Being safe also means living without fear of rejection or punishment, or living in survival mode, cloistered in our towers afraid to come out. Retribution means you feel punished for what you say or do. Your feelings are not respected. I call them "punishing dynamics." These dynamics are often the passive side of conversing, like nonengagement, pouting, or silent treatment. We are all familiar with these and others we learned at home, and will make them part of our new home without work, patience, and grace.

When the castle is secure, we are empowered to find what we need for love and life together. We secure our castle as we learn to edit or remove dishonoring from our dynamics—meaning that we deal with how we behave within ourselves by repenting. This means we choose not to continue to do it, but commit to growing out of our baby attitudes that are selfish, sinful, and degrading. We die to ourselves and grow up, no longer permitting ourselves to be bullied or abusive in speech or attitude.

Our marriages are made up of how we treat each other and the interpersonal dynamics we create. It's not *the marriage,* as some impersonal entity—it's _us_, the personally broken ones who are making it what it is. These are the nuts and bolts of what makes up a *bad marriage,* which is in reality what we are *doing* to each other.

Securing the castle from within—engaging with each other, operating in trust and unity—means we are better prepared to fight the dragons and pirates that could attack us from without.

So how do we secure our castles from within?

Secure Your Castle with Covenant

We start at the altar when we speak our marriage vows to each other before God and witnesses. We often hear the promise to *love, honor, and protect,* followed by the words *till death do you part.* What does this covenant mean?

We are stating that no matter what, we won't bail out on our covenant and our promise to each other by leaving the relationship. We aren't safe if we are willing to throw our covenant away or threaten abandonment in the marriage. We aren't safe if we don't keep our word.

It's easy to make the vow and say the words in the flush of new love with the love drugs in our bloodstream. Where did those come from by the way, and how can I get a refill on that prescription? I guess I need to see the doctor. The words we promised in our vows are more easily forgotten when the marriage has polarized us and the traits that attracted us now push us away from each other isolating us in our towers.

Linda shares her experiences at the beginning of our marriage:

> When I married Dan, I brought a powerful relational tool I had used in previous relationships: "If you don't like it, you can leave."
> My history in the face of conflict and struggle was to keep my mouth shut until I could stand it no longer. Then I would announce, "I want a divorce."
> I did not have the tools to make a marriage work, so I employed the only recourse I could figure out which was to abandon ship.
> As we sought help early in our marriage, our counselor explained that we needed a safety fence around our marriage. We needed to create a safe place to work through conflict and build our relationship. My part in creating a safe place was to change my conviction that one of us could leave if it didn't work out. My vows had to go deeper than my lifelong conviction

that I could bail out if I didn't like it. I was going to have to learn how to hang in there, no matter what it took.

I, Dan, remember the first time Linda said, "If you don't like it, you can leave."

My response was simply, "I'm not going anywhere." I didn't marry her just to bail out when the going got rough. I thought, *We've got to work this out – figure it out.*

I knew I had problems. I also knew God was squeezing her and exposing stuff to heal her, and I needed to stand strong. I was surprised at how quickly she took out the big gun of abandonment, but knew she had a painful relational history, and this was her pain surfacing. She hadn't learned any healthy ways of handling conflict.

She was testing our limits. I feared abandonment and didn't want her to leave. At the same time, God gave me grace and courage as I reached out to him for answers and strategies. He gave me the grace to be the beach for her waves to crash on. (I read that somewhere, thank you.)

He taught me how to trust him with her and the marriage. We both needed healing, and a lot of brokenness was surfacing. Many issues needed unpacking, and I knew she was hurting as much as I was. I had to trust God with the process.

Abandoning the relationship wasn't an option for me. I wouldn't let her throw me out either. She was going to have to deal with me. I was still learning to manage the emotions of conflict, but I knew abandonment by either of us wasn't an option. There was simply nowhere to go but ahead.

We needed to remember our covenant to one another, stay the course, and allow God to love us, help us, and heal us.

And he did.

But my point is, that your first line of defense is *not leaving*. I've often thought of this marriage safety fence as a boxing ring that allows you to work out conflict without leaving the contest. You may bounce off the ropes, but no one leaves the ring. No one is going anywhere. This provides security; this is securing our castles.

Going back to the castle metaphor, the moat is intact. No one is going to swim away.

Secure Your Castle with Emotional Safety

An important part of safeguarding your castle is making it a safe place to be. One of the questions in the State of the Union Evaluation found in the study guide in the back of the book asks, "How safe do you feel opening up to your partner?"

Most of us don't spend much time thinking about how safe we are or feel. However, as soon as we enter relationships, *how safe we feel* immediately defines our relationship. We aren't about to open up and throw everything out there until we feel safe doing so. How we respond to shared truth from our partner proves whether we are safe or not. The intimacy of our marriages depends on our ability to create emotional safety for each spouse. We need it because emotional safety is our security system. It's the bridge to emotional honesty and intimacy, which is foundational to building a stronger marriage.

Nothing can happen without it, because our hearts won't stay open to each other unless our shared feelings and emotions are treated with honor, respect, and validation. Vulnerability must be protected and nurtured. This is the holy ground where our corporate history of trust and safety is developed and grown throughout our marriage.

I like how Gary Smalley explains it:

> Security enables us to truly open up and be known at a deep, intimate level without fear of being blamed, criticized, judged, or condemned. — The only way to create this kind of marital intimacy is to focus significant time, attention, and energy on creating an environment in which both partners feel secure in each other's love and acceptance when they make themselves vulnerable by opening up. Security reduces the risk.[1]

Marriage Beginners

Early in our marriages, when broken patterns surface, our home doesn't feel like a safe place, and for good reason. Most of us haven't dealt with emotional intensity at this level and haven't learned skills to navigate it safely. It feels unpredictable and unsafe.

Linda and I had mentors in our early years together, from whom we learned about communication dynamics, words, and the relational messages we were sending to each other. We were able to identify issues by doing our homework, practicing, and removing destructive, sabotaging ways from our talking. Active listening skills aided us in hearing and honoring feelings and issues without defensiveness. We could get past barriers that always tripped us up in the past. Many couples confess communication is their number one barrier. If you can't talk right you can't fight right.

As beginners in our marriages, when we're honest with each other, there will be some collateral damage. Even spouses who love each other deeply can react unwisely. There can be anger, invalidation, or criticism that tempts us to close our hearts to each other from that moment on. These feelings will diminish as we secure our castles with safety.

Linda and I both brought broken patterns into our marriage, as all people do. This caused a lot of sparks to fly, threatening to set our house afire. There were tense, anxious times as our conflicts developed. We didn't know yet that God was behind these conflicts and was using them to expose, and then heal us of our brokenness.

Early Fights

Because of our wounded pasts and poor modeling growing up, we hadn't learned to fight fairly or honor others when we disagreed. Our early fights were painful because we didn't know how to do it right. But God met us in our pain and confusion, gave us grace together, and taught us. Our safety fence held.

At first, we didn't know how to use diplomacy, negotiate, or flex because we felt so threatened. We were reacting rather than responding. We hadn't built our security system, so honesty or conflict created pain and chaos. It was more of a war zone than a safety one. We created this chaos through our inability to listen, wrong use of words, and attitudes that were unaccepting, threatening, and blaming.

Defensiveness

Early in our marriage, there were lots of attacks going on. I think I felt attacked more than she did since she has a stronger personality. The insecurity of the man mentioned in the two towers was strong in me, and I had several reactions:

- I felt defensive and under attack.
- I felt performance pain like I was "not measuring up" most of the time.
- I thought I had to rescue and fix things (which I couldn't), and this raised my anxiety.

To make matters worse, her inviting me to leave wasn't bolstering my manly feelings of courage and confidence. I was looking for my sword, and the scabbard was empty. This stuff is harder on guys than women realize.

Until we learn to fight fairly and accept and honor feelings, we are prone to attack and bully our spouses while defending ourselves. It could be a form of self-protection because we don't yet feel accepted, validated, or understood. It's probably the reason early conflicts are so feisty when we wonder if we'll make it. As we will show, the safety we need for our security is cultivated.

Fighting fair is *not* natural and is a discipline learned and practiced. Many of us didn't see it at home and sure didn't learn it in school. Premarital counseling was the first place I saw it, and little did I know the ride we would be in for. To this day, I marvel at how hard it is to lay down defensiveness and learn to actively listen to another person.

But that's exactly what I needed to do— overcome my defensiveness and try to find Linda's heart. I was unable to hear her heart while protecting mine. I had to stop fighting for my safety through defending, and learn to hear her, then validate and honor her feelings.

This was the start of my journey into self-awareness as I began to see the dynamics I was creating. God helped me yield my pain to him and showed me what I was doing.

He would catch me in the act and show me my defensiveness was the problem. He said, *We can't get past this until you surrender it, let it go.* Pride needed to go so humility could come, so I *owned* my defensiveness. I had to trust God with my heart instead of self-protecting. I realized that the process of securing the castle is letting God expose and deal with insecurity.

I wrote the following poem reflecting on a time when my heart felt wounded, longing to trust but needing safety too. I think this question is universal to all wounded hearts.

Can I Trust You?
Can I trust you with my heart and the things that are inside?
Will you accept me for who I am, or will I run and hide?
I know things about myself, not sure it's safe to share.
It hurts when I'm mishandled, I need love and tender care.

Can I trust you with my heart, to tell you how I feel?
Will you handle what I tell you and love me till I heal?
I really want to trust you and make you my safe place,
Knowing you won't judge me, but only give me grace.

Show me I can trust you and run to you at last,
To overcome my hurts and betrayals from the past.
I opened up my heart to them, risking all to love,
But only got it broken with rejection and a shove.

I really want to trust you with all that's in my soul.
You can help me trust with love that makes me whole.
A love that's unconditional without its harsh demands.
One that understands me, with kind and gentle hands.

A patient love that listens, accepting every part,
Is a love that holds the mercy to heal my broken heart.

Secure Your Castle by Learning Your Relational DNA

Every couple develops relating patterns that come out of who we are together. This is the relational DNA that forms the way we talk and respond to each other. This DNA creates our dynamics or the energy that fuels our cause-and-effect reactions. In our marriages, our brokenness and pain will find each other.

This relational DNA is discovered through our conflicts. We will fight about our broken places and the needs flowing out of them. The conflict becomes redemptive as we uncover the wounds God seeks to heal. Through this healing process, we explore, discover, and bond over intimate areas of our hearts and connect through understanding and validation. This is the process of our hearts knowing and being known.

When our honeymoon feelings faded and our differences were magnified, we saw how broken we were with little to bring to the table. Linda and I developed dysfunctional, destructive, and dishonoring dynamics. Neither of us listened well, and we both used power in wrong ways We were stubborn, and both fought to be right, understood, and to win our way. We didn't have a *bad marriage*; we had bad dynamics. Gradually, we developed skills that enabled us to talk to and listen to each other well and secure our castle.

Doing the Work

But it doesn't "just happen." In one sense, we are responsible for breaking the spell that gets us out of the tower. Yes, God frees us, but only as we co-operate and do our part. The hurtful patterns we practice in marriage won't change until we own our stuff. Nothing can change until we take responsibility for what we are creating. Things won't improve until we can say the words, "Yes, I see I'm doing that and it's hurting us. I want to work on that so we can grow and change."

Imagine a marriage as a dance, with both partners taking broken steps that impact the rhythm of the other. To find our rhythm together, berating or blaming our partner— stepping on their toes doesn't help. Instead, each partner needs to concentrate on relearning his or her broken steps. It's the "power of one," as Michael and Amy Smalley call it. "When your own growth—not changing your spouse—is your goal, you won't fail."[2]

When I take responsibility for what I am doing, I am empowered to change. When I don't, I remain a victim of the dynamics I helped create, complaining about my bad marriage when I am responsible for half of the steps.

Nothing is more discouraging than longing for relief in a marriage to someone who doesn't want to do the work to see the marriage grow. A good marriage takes a mutual commitment to

- grow out of immaturity and selfishness into mature, selfless love
- do the work of engaging, resolving issues, and breaking painful patterns
- refuse to sweep things under the rug and hide behind "business as usual"

The bottom line is that refusing to engage in conflict leads to a cool, disconnected climate and often evolves into being nonsexual, at least not with your spouse.

M. Scott Peck says in *The Road Less Traveled*, "The number one impediment to spiritual growth is laziness. If we overcome laziness, all other impediments will be overcome."[3]

In light of this, without being oversimplistic, loss of joy and lingering marriage problems most often stem from the reality that people don't want to own their stuff—or take responsibility for their sins and brokenness. They don't want to do the work it takes to dismantle the power struggle and grow together— they want to blame and control.

Yes, it's hard, but real love will do the work and take the risks. The quest for happily ever after leads down the path of spiritual growth and personal responsibility. A strong marriage is built on a covenant that is *demonstrated* by an all-in commitment (Heb. 6:11–12).

Secure Your Castle by Practicing the Rules of Engagement

This is where we begin to edit the broken patterns causing our problems. Unless we examine our broken patterns—and take responsibility for putting a stop to them—nothing will change. We will stay victims of what we do to each other.

So how do we begin? Identify the pain behind why you respond the way you do. Broken patterns might be rooted in past hurts, but they are practiced and reinforced daily by our current words and actions. I met with a man some years back and he told me, "Other people don't cause you pain—they are touching your pain."

My spouse isn't causing me pain; she is touching my pain. I've brought my wounds, fears, and broken patterns in, and she's finding them all. She isn't causing my pain, but she is touching it by pushing my buttons and getting my broken reactions from me. She's my mirror.

I created the Rules of Engagement, (found in the study guide at the back of the book), to help couples recognize the words and actions sabotaging their marriage and to make better choices—or halt the process until those better choices can be made. This is a tool that provides structure around our relating patterns so we can corral them and be responsible for what we do to each other.

For example, one of the Rules of Engagement is *I will not raise my voice or yell at you.* If I break this rule, the conversation stops until I can control my anger and agree not to raise my voice. Easier said than done, I know, but it does work with practice, and relief comes.

This is where "owning your stuff and doing the work" comes into play. It means being willing to say, "Yes, I see where my anger is interfering with our process and hurting you. I choose to commit to us by digging into the pain behind my anger and dealing with it instead of punishing you with it."

In other words, this is where I commit to spiritual growth instead of clinging to my immature relating. I will choose to grow out of this childish thing.

We long to connect but can't because of what we do to each other. Our broken communication styles and words keep us in our towers and we can't connect.

When we stop blowing up our communication bridges, the path to intimacy opens to us. This brings us hope because it puts us in charge of our dynamics. Instead of hurting ourselves, we can love each other to life. It is a discipline we need, or we won't change.

Secure Your Castle by Courageously Surrendering to Each Other

"Mutual submission is the only workable path to a strong marriage."[4]

How can two hearts become one unless they are submitted to one another? We can't experience marriage in its fullness unless we're willing to surrender to each other. Without risking this yielding, we aren't giving our hearts away to our spouse. Everything else is just more information unless we get this right. We cannot escape the power struggle without submission and humility — we will continue to fight over the power. Mutual submission is the core marriage heart posture that connects a couple intimately for life.

A Fresh Look at Submission

"Do not be unwise, but understand what the will of the Lord is . . . submitting to one another in the fear of God" (Eph. 5:17, 21).

True submission is given; it can't be taken. No one can make you submit. That is domination or control. Authentic submission has nothing to do with the power of another controlling you or making your choices for you. That is called subjugation.

Submission is *not* about one having the power to tell another person what to do. Try to see submission as a quality chosen, rather than another having a position of power.

I know there's abuse, and I advise men or women who are in abusive marriages to seek a safe place and get counseling. I'm aware submission is a trigger word, but we can't avoid talking about and clarifying it. If the truth isn't revealed, we can't move into it.

Whenever submission is demanded of another, what the other gives is not submission. This is because their freedom to choose has been violated. That is subjugation. Whenever it is demanded, it can no longer be submitted. It has already been taken or rather violated.

What if what we long for so deeply can only be obtained by cooperating with and yielding to our spouses? What if it can only be found by obeying God's directive to surrender, yield, and submit to each other?

Becoming one doesn't mean we lose ourselves. We don't lose our power or freedom to choose as individuals. God never takes that from us. Instead, we make decisions about what we are going to do with that power and freedom in the context of our marriage. It's an environment of freedom, humility, and surrender where love can grow and deepen. There is nothing of coercion or the use of power present when submitting to another.

The beauty of submission is seen between two lovers when they choose freely to honor each other out of an act of love, rather than a duty, obligation, or mandate. There is no pressure, manipulation, or retribution involved.

Conflict and submission are often found in the same arena as we find our way. The only way to resolve most conflicts is to submit to one another. We submit to our spouses whenever we make the choice to honor another's desire and lay ours down—or at least enter into respectful negotiation together to reach an agreement. I submit when I listen without defending. I bring my feelings and fears to the cross and trust God with the outcome.

We submit to the mirror of our spouses when they speak the truth to us. We can then acknowledge the truth about what is being shown and seen, and we can choose to submit ourselves to the truth. We can do this when we are not being shamed or condemned by them.

When a marriage is founded on mutual submission, we lose our self-serving agendas and gain freedom. We lose the anxiety and strife we feel and gain depth in the relationship instead.

If surrendering to each other sounds challenging, don't worry. We're going to learn how to do this in the next chapter.

CHAPTER SIX

Win the Power Challenge

Control can look aggressive like a T-Rex or passive like a lamb, but in either case, the root problem is the same — fear.

— Danny Silk

We win the power challenge in our marriages by learning how to use power corporately. This means we share the power — giving and taking in how we use power so that both spouses feel respected and honored. Neither spouse is trying to power the other one down. This doesn't come naturally as many of us have been trained to get what we want through whatever means necessary. Once again, our histories develop our patterns of how we use power; we're used to them, and they don't change easily.

The road to connection and the intimacy we crave runs through the power struggles and how we handle them, one challenge at a time. This means we learn not to bully or cave in without being assertive and develop fair representation in our relating. We gain this strength as we engage the conflicts around the use of power in our relationship. We live in a must-win, competitive culture where everyone in a conflict feels compelled to win. When we bring this attitude into marriage, we create relational inequality where one person won't feel emotionally safe, known, or cherished. When winning is more important than loving, you will both lose.

My early experience with Linda wasn't fighting over power, but rather fighting against not having any. There was only one powerful person in the relationship, and it wasn't me. I had to overcome powerlessness and my lack of ability to be assertive and represent myself. Later, when I gained the strength to enter the contest with her, then we had conflicts over who had the power and how it was being used.

I first heard the phrase "level the playing field" from a counselor who had just listened to me share the dynamics I was having early in my marriage to Linda. I felt put down, and powerless to assert myself or express my opinions, desires, and needs. He said, "You've given her all the power. You need to level the playing field in your marriage. By not asserting yourself, you're not getting fair representation at the table. You need to learn how to assert yourself and express your opinions, desires, and needs in the face of a stronger personality." Then he added, "Without caving in."

Without caving in? (That's all I ever saw Dad do).

"In addition to being assertive—and honest—you have to be willing to engage her in the challenge and even conflict."

Having never seen this, it seemed impossible to me as I lacked the skills and fortitude to stand up strong and represent myself with confidence.

When one spouse uses more power than the other unchallenged, the stronger one can bully and rule the relationship and control the dynamics to their benefit. When this happens, the weaker spouse is degraded and won't feel heard, honored, or respected. The weaker one loses their place at the negotiating table because they can't show up with a voice. The marriage becomes lopsided and intimacy is out of reach since you can't degrade your spouse and be intimate with them at the same time.

If there is an imbalance, the couple won't know what it feels like to connect heart to heart. This imbalance of power exists in many couples dynamics who don't realize it, or fear to address the issue of power. These marriages don't operate as a united front, lacking the power that agreement and honoring bring. When domination and fear rule, they can't validate feelings and desires which leads to the enjoyment of a connected relationship.

It's best to level the playing field early in a marriage since you are forming the relational patterns and dynamics that will impact you for years to come. Repeating patterns reinforced through repetition cement our dynamics. When we can see our power imbalance early and see where we are degrading, we can do something about whatever becomes clear, and connect better.

How each partner uses power determines whether your dynamics will connect you or not. It's not much of a marriage if one passive personality gets snuffed out, suppressed, or eclipsed by a stronger, more dominant one.

In our case, Linda possessed the power, and I didn't because of my broken masculinity and history (my tower). This didn't necessarily make her a bully, but rather a steamroller who ran over my lack of initiative and confidence. She wasn't going to become weaker in the face of my inability to engage. She was going to be who she was—strong and confident. While I was being tentative and steamrolled, she was a confident, powerful woman, waiting for me to show up.

Is that all you've got? she seemed to be saying.

The good news is that eventually, I did show up, but it required me to unpack the reasons behind my tentativeness and address them. There is pain and wounding in this arena that strips us of our identity and our power, and this quest takes time with God's healing love to find wholeness.

I can't imagine this process without God, who reveals our brokenness to us, and the reasons behind it, then lovingly heals and empowers us. Jesus truly is the hero of our stories who joins us in this delicate process of balancing power.

This leveling of our playing field was our spiritual journey and a necessity for us to learn mutual respect and how to honor. We leveled through the conflicts that helped us discover what we were doing to each other.

Typically in a relationship, one must come down, while the other comes up to find a balance that works for honoring both. Power can and does disconnect us when a powerful one dominates the other. One is not meant to rule the roost, not in a happy and fulfilled marriage. Power struggles drain the positive energy of a marriage and degrade. The power needs to be shared for us to experience life-giving pools of intimacy and nurture.

It helps to talk about how you use power, make decisions, and how you both feel about its use. This will protect you from escalation and ensure you are both heard well and can honor what you are hearing. Everything feels better when you can listen to each other actively, and validate.

"Yes, I hear what you're saying."

Early in marriage, it takes practice before you can talk respectfully, listen well, and validate—especially when insecurity, ego, and defensiveness are present.

Spouses can learn to be assertive in healthy ways to ensure the opinions, thoughts, and feelings of both are being honored. This is critical for mutual connection. Without it, we'll never get out of our respective towers. The one with all the power has the keys until the other gains theirs and the field is leveled. Then the keys are on one key chain, and you can both use them.

Needs won't be mutually met, and feelings and values won't be unpacked and honored together if one person is the boss and the other follows along without voice or input. You may let them call all the shots without contesting because you lack the power to be assertive, but you will feel empty like something is missing.

It helps to see that this submitted position of the weaker one isn't a position another is enforcing over you, but rather one you are assuming by your lack of personal representation and expression of what you need and who you are. This is the position of a powerless person or victim. The stronger, dominant one can be a man or a woman, depending on personality development and relational history.

How Did I Get Here? Where Did My Power Go?

This lopsided balance of power was our situation and why the counselor told me I needed to speak up as an empowered person and stop letting Linda roll over me as if I was a *nonentity*; one not worth considering.

First I needed to discover why I felt unable to stand up. I had to ask, *Why am I letting her bully me?*

Truth is, I originally lost my power to the dysfunction in my family; our family of origin shapes who we are and who we become as adults. We lose our power in a disempowering environment when there are no healthy boundaries established, and yours are invaded. We lose our power when the security, love, and validation we need as children are not present in our childhood.

Thank You!

I am grateful to Mom and Dad for the love and support they provided for us eight kids, and I honor the memory of them. I take responsibility for who I am and my brokenness and don't blame them or harbor unforgiveness or bitterness. However, I need to be honest about what my heart experienced, what shaped me, and why during my formative years, or I will stay in denial of my heart's condition. They both sacrificed to provide for us and care for our needs. We always had food on the table, a roof over our heads, and a place called home, even though it didn't feel emotionally safe and secure.

Sure, they loved me, but there were love deficits my heart experienced that shaped the adult me. These are the inner healing areas God wants to access in my heart to heal. My parents never divorced in sixty years of marriage, even though there were turbulent times and many conflicts that weren't resolved.

I will share now some of their stories that created the DNA of our upbringing. See if you can find any of your stories in what I share or can identify with the feelings and struggles I faced. May the empowering road of my quest become yours.

My Father's Story

Dad was an only child and deserted by a father he never knew and was raised by his mom and an aunt. This desertion by his father was an expression of broken masculinity. Men who abandon their wives and children are broken and live to serve their own selfish or sexual interests. Rather, whole men protect their wives and children and fight for their lives and hearts.

I share this about Dad's upbringing to show he didn't inherit a model of whole masculinity from his father, but rather a broken one. He was raised by women. Thank God they were there for him, but his father was absent, robbing the development he could have received as a boy growing into manhood. There was no man there to call him out during the vulnerable, critical years of adolescence in a young man's life when a boy needs a father to bond with. A man to show him the ropes so to speak; one who can impart the courage to be assertive, and take the initiative to face the world and life's challenges with strength and authority. This is what masculine strength brings.

If the masculine role model is missing, the boy is in trouble. Lacking the strength and guidance of the father, a vacuum is left inside the emerging boy, and he is unable to break away from the mother-son bond and become a man—fully masculine and able to give himself to his wife with strength.

Gordon Dalbey, in *Healing the Masculine Soul*, says,

> When a boy reaches puberty, filled with the powerful stirrings of his emerging manhood, the father's role becomes critical. If the boy at this point is not called out and away from the mother by the father, those stirrings are overtaken by his natural physical bond with his mother, becoming bound up in her and thus unavailable later to the woman he might love.[1]

Perhaps this is why God gave Adam and Eve Genesis 2:24: "Therefore a man shall leave his father and mother and be joined to his wife and they shall become one flesh."

God, the Father calls a young man out and away from his idolatrous dependence upon the woman to tell him he's a man. He must leave mommy—and the mommy figures he has become dependent upon. He must find himself, to become whole so he can cleave to his wife. This is harder for a boy to do in the chaos that's created when mom is in charge, controlling the boy and his development while dad is passive and absent. He needs his dad to *call him out* by modeling masculine assertiveness and initiative. More than ever in today's confused model of gender, masculine leadership and initiative are not available.

It seems that the doorways to idolatry and sexual addiction are opened here—when the boy can't break his mom's possessive grip and individuate to become a man. Without masculine leadership, a young man is not taught how to manage his sexuality. These doors of idolatry are closed only when the man repents of bending to the woman, and returns to God the Father to empower him to stand up and be a man. I have found the fathering of God to be the tenderest, most empowering experience of my life.

I remember Dad telling me how much he'd craved a masculine role model, but none was there for him. He spoke lovingly of his grandfather he would spend summers with, fishing and exploring. They were the best times of his childhood.

In the absence of a role model, Dad was not *called out* in a masculine sense. He could not be assertive and personally powerful because there was no man to teach him. Therefore, he was unable to impart to his four sons the confidence and ability to stand up as men. You can't pass on what you didn't receive or haven't seen.

Dad abdicated his strength creating a power imbalance. When a void is created by this imbalance, a woman will flow into it. She thinks, *If he won't take the initiative, I will.*

Some women may say, "What's wrong with that?" But the honest ones know that any power imbalance weakens a marriage. They will admit that they want their man to stand up and be a man, stand toe to toe with her, represent himself, and not be a pushover. She wants him to show masculine initiative, show up with an opinion, and fight for it, in a good way, instead of caving into her strength or challenge. Research revealed by women shows that when they reach for his strength, they want to find some.

Dalby, in *Healing the Masculine Soul*, in chapter 4 entitled "She Left Me!" unpacks at length, with expert quotes and various personal testimonies, the fact that a woman wants a strong man to stand up to. He says that in our overreacting to the "macho male image," many men have become desensitized, have gone soft, and are unable to engage their women in conflict or difference of opinion and stand their ground.[2]

A man will either move into his masculine role and shape the chaos created by life, his family, or his spouse, or he will be ruled by it. In the case of a woman being powered down, or bullied by a dominant male, she needs to level the playing field in her own right and learn to stand up to *his* chaos and be assertive.

Don't stumble over the gender issue, as power ignores gender. This isn't about a man dominating a woman because she's a woman. I'm a man, and I was ruled over by women all my life until I took responsibility for what *I* was doing. I was abdicating my manhood to gain from her the approval I didn't receive as a child. I needed to stand next to her as an equal, not to dominate but to share power equally so we could be stronger together as a couple. She needed my strength when I found it as much as I needed hers.

This isn't about the sword between the sexes. It's a personality issue and is fueled by the interplay between power and dysfunction, and it can only be addressed and solved by mutual submission in marriage. This removes the power struggle—not that it goes away forever. Occasional tests and conflicts will come to humble us and keep us growing. Surrendering to each other instead of dominating and fighting for power is the pathway to peace, connection, and intimacy.

This is God's kingdom path to healing.

We can't use wounds and abuse in our past as an excuse to not deal with our issues today. Instead, as we submit to

God and each other, God wants to heal those wounds so we can escape our towers and experience a fulfilling relationship. We can become secure in ourselves and don't have to broker power to protect ourselves or try to gain from another what we should be going to God for.

My Mother's Story

My mother's father wasn't around her family much, and he didn't sound like a father who was present at home, engaged, or bringing strength to his family. Family lore has it that he rode with Pancho Villa and would go south from Arizona and disappear into the Sonoran Desert in Mexico for months at a time. Then, when my mother was sixteen, her father died tragically in a fiery traffic accident on Thanksgiving night.

My mother had to grow up fast when her mother then abandoned the family, leaving Mom to raise her younger siblings during the depression years. She later became involved with us grandkids, loved us dearly, and nurtured us until she died. She helped buffer us from the chaos created by my mom's anger. I remember one time she grabbed the belt out of Mom's hand and talked her down. Grandma would say, "Now, Judy, we don't need that belt. They're just being kids."

It was a terrible loss for me when she died during surgery unexpectedly when I was in my early teens.

Who will replace that source of nurture in my heart? I worried.

Because circumstances called for it growing up, Mom developed a strong, self-sufficient, independent personality, leaving no room for negotiation or compromise. It was my way or the highway, take no prisoners, and show no mercy when it came to who held the power.

She moved into the vacuum of power Dad created by not bringing his strength to bear on us eight kids. To his credit, he did have "family meetings," trying to bring order and tell us how it was going to be. He would walk around the house clapping his hands, gathering us up, declaring, "Meeting, meeting, family meeting!"

And we would dutifully assemble and listen, but we knew it was futile. We all knew who the incumbent president was — who was in office. The belt Mom yielded was the final rule of the day, with or without the meetings. Dad did try, though.

With Mom, there were rules to be kept or punishment would follow. She struggled with depression and often was not emotionally available. I know now that she was in emotional pain. Seeing her history, you can see why. When she was emotionally expressive, the dominant emotion was anger.

Growing up at home, there was no reasoning or negotiating with her that ever worked. We weren't allowed to express emotions or process them out loud. You stuffed them or you were given "something to cry about." A lot was bottled up. Life hurt, and there was nowhere to process it.

Power Imbalance

We watched Mom dominate Dad while wielding all the power. All the fights we saw involved her anger pushing him into "submission" with violent, degrading words. We learned to withdraw from conflict and surrender power quickly to avoid injury from the excessive power of another — my mother. We lost our respective power and had no grid for what healthy boundaries look like. This left us disempowered and unable to assert ourselves or represent strength. You either grow into confident powerful people, or insecure victims unable to represent themselves with strength. The family of origin determines this.

Once, Mom kicked Dad out. He came home from work and found all his belongings on the front porch and was locked out of the house as well. We endured the trauma of watching her angrily throw all his stuff out. As I look back, that didn't seem like fighting fair. She was using rejection and abandonment to win the power struggle. That teaches little hearts what to expect if you stand up to power. You'll get thrown out—or abandoned, just like Dad did.

I was little and don't remember the details, but I do remember that Dad moved into a hotel room and stayed away for a while. I didn't have visiting privileges.

She'd always take him back, but the balance of power never shifted upon his return. There would be a brief honeymoon period before the cycle would repeat itself, but we were grateful they were still together. It didn't feel safe and secure because who knew when she would throw him out again? I carried this helpless, tentative, disempowered feeling into adulthood.

My Story

In my first marriage, I was unable to stand up and be a man. I needed the approval and affirmation she couldn't give. Now I was scared and insecure moving into marriage with Linda. I lacked the masculine strength and security to stand equally with her and challenge her strength, which seemed formidable. I believed she loved me, but her attitude expressed a superiority that her opinions, wisdom, and judgments made mine unworthy of being taken seriously.

Mommy will show you what to do. We don't need to be concerned with your point of view. Mommy knows best.

She never said those words to me, but subconsciously, it's what I painfully felt, and I was degraded by it. My lack of confidence and courage were connected to wounds from my childhood, and I felt unequipped to navigate and thrive in my relationship with this powerful woman. It was easy to believe that I didn't have what it took because I didn't! This truth was locking me in the tower.

I felt like Gru in *Despicable Me* as the little boy with the rocket. Every time he built something bigger and better, it was never enough to get his mom's approval. Nothing I could do would ever be enough. *I'm not equipped for this*, I would often think. I have found in my reading that many men carry this refrain. It's part of the lie that puts men in their towers that says, *You aren't equipped for this.* And maybe at the start, we aren't, but this is where God shows up with his fathering presence to equip us and remove our shame.

It takes two people to create relational dynamics, (our cause and effect relating). In our marriage, it was partly what she was doing, but it was my passivity and lack of masculine strength that was creating my submitted dynamic. I wasn't showing up, so my lack of power let hers move into my void. Without my vote, she made the decision each time one needed to be made.

Of course, it's always a lopsided arrangement when it's time for your needs, desires, and opinions to be heard or validated. She wasn't listening to those things, and I was unable and afraid to express them. The issue wasn't that we fought over who had the power (I didn't have any); the issue was how she was treating me in degrading ways that were dishonoring me. She didn't respect me as a man or even as a person and didn't try to hide it. There was degrading going on, and I felt it and knew it wasn't right. This is ultimately what brought me to the counselor.

I needed approval, so I performed for Linda for love. This came from a core belief that if I did anything she didn't like or approve of (including disagreeing with or challenging her), she'd stop loving me, or possibly abandon me.

I wasn't in touch with that belief until God showed me it was paralyzing me from relating to her in confident, healthy ways. I was looking to her to *make me enough* instead of going to God to *be enough*. He exposed the approval addiction that was controlling me, locking me in my tower. I was afraid of her rejecting or abandoning me, so I abdicated and gave away my strength.

It's the retreat of the broken masculine. When a woman reaches for the heart of her man in this case, there's nothing there for her. He won't say what he wants and needs because he's not in touch, and too busy protecting himself from failing or being abandoned. Fearing conflict, he can't unpack the truth and nothing gets resolved. He can't and won't give her anything to work with.

Dalbey says, concerning men,

> For our own part, we may well fear the woman's initiative because it reminds us of our own lack of it. In fact, the degree to which a man fears the woman's initiative may be a primary indicator of the extent to which he has not offered himself

to Jesus and sought the Father God's initiative. This, of course, requires letting go of the mother/woman as the source of life.[3]

In my journey, I couldn't see what I was doing. I could only feel the pain that caused me to retreat from Linda because she couldn't affirm and validate me. I didn't know that I was afraid of her until God showed me. I didn't know that I feared her disapproval, and was holding back from her. I wasn't aware that I was looking to her, or other female goddesses as my source of life. God brought me to that realization, and I saw the bondage associated with it. I then repented and found freedom and empowering to be a man apart from what a woman could give me.

I heard John Eldridge, author of *Wild at Heart*, say at a Love and War Marriage Conference years ago that "a man who fears his wife will give away his masculinity."

This pierced my heart and I saw that I was still fearing my wife, looking to her for approval, and to tell me I was a man. I was still performing for her love in areas, instead of trusting God with my heart and risking truth-telling even if it meant challenge, confrontation, and conflict.

I didn't want to take this risk, but God was calling me to do it out of obedience to him and because it's what my wife needed. It's what *we* needed. It takes two empowered people to have a healthy relationship.

Raising the Sword of Assertiveness

We slay the dragon of fear when we take empowered risks to be assertive.

This means risking emotional honesty, standing up, and stating how you feel and what you want, in the face of disagreement. You stop cowering back in fear of the outcome that enables a form of emotional abuse against you.

I felt God's affirmation as I began to stand up for myself. I saw that standing up was something *he wanted* me to do. I would just as soon have stayed safely silent in the shadows performing for love as I'd always done. It was obedience to him when I resisted the degradation I felt, repented of abdication, and started asserting myself. I wasn't glorifying God as a man by being a pushover; I glorified him when I moved into my strength, instead of fearing it.

In the same way I learned to exercise my strength, you, as a woman, bring glory to God by establishing healthy boundaries with your man. Submission is not subjugation, where you feel oppressed and resentful. What I am saying is that God's will does not call us into a degraded place of unhealthy submission. He calls us to move out of that and honor one another.

We are not victims to be ordered around, lacking power or representation. As a woman, you need to be honored and valued equal to your man. You deserve respect for your opinions and ideas. Both spouses must be willing to submit to each other (1 Peter 3:1, 7).

Assertion Defined

The key to submitting to one another is found in both partners asserting themselves. This is the way to a corporate sharing of power. I looked up what it means "to assert oneself." It means to appear or show up, to come forth or take a stand, to stand up and be counted, to speak out, to raise one's voice, to speak one's mind, or to draw attention to oneself.

In other words, when you are assertive, you represent yourself through your God-given personality.

You don't exist as a codependent nonentity without opinions or influence. God never created anyone to do that. We can't reflect his glory when our expression of personality is suppressed. God doesn't squash our personalities or subjugate us. He never takes away a person's free will, nor should we.

God doesn't take people over, control, suppress them, or edit their personalities. He transforms what we willingly give to him. Neither can we take away the free will of our spouse by trying to take over, change them, or dominate them.

Leveling the Playing Field

When the counselor told me I needed to "level the playing field" with Linda, he was talking about how quickly I was giving my power away. He also talked about my need to respect myself and my dignity. He said there needed to be this thing inside me that said, *How dare you treat me that way!* I took abusive treatment because I was unable to contest the violation of my boundaries. I needed to learn to respect myself, value who I was, and stand up for the things I should.

When I was being degraded or bullied, I needed to do these things to level the playing field:

1. Place a higher value on my perspectives and views of things.
2. Give me permission to stand up and be counted.
3. Believe that my thoughts and opinions deserve equal consideration and respect.
4. Fight to be heard, honored, and respected, and dig in and resist when I wasn't.

In time, I learned to "stand in there" without crumbling beneath the force of her personality. I also started speaking up when I felt I wasn't being honored and valued and courageously stepped into the conflict. For example, I permitted myself to say things like"This is unfair; you can't just decide that without including me in the process. It's not okay for you to commit me and my time to something without getting my agreement first" or "I don't feel like you are honoring my opinion or point of view. You are discounting it and bullying me. This isn't fair. Do you see what you're doing?"

My emerging strength became a mirror she had to face that exposed how she was degrading me while she "ran" the marriage in a dishonoring way.

From Fear to Faith

There was a shifting of the balance of power in our dynamics as I shed my victim role, took responsibility, and repented for my idolatry and fear of man. God was raising me to share the power with her.

He didn't take hers away; he restored mine, which empowered us both through balance.

As I found my voice and power, it created space for us to unpack our struggles and look for solutions. These were honoring conversations as I "stood up" and gave us both something to work with. I learned to find my voice, which I hadn't dared to use before out of fear.

Linda learned what honor and respect for a man looked like, and was willing to learn with me. I respected her and showed her how to respect me in return by sharing how I felt when she did and said degrading things. I'd never been able to do this, with inadequacy ruling my roost. This moved our hearts closer together, as mutual respect does, and allowed her to change with me.

It took time and perseverance, but we learned to fight fair and honor each other's feelings. We learned active listening and validation skills (These are found in the study guide for chapter 7), and used these tools to go deeper than either of us had gone before in a relationship. Our sabotaging ways were exposed and ended.

We both changed how we treated each other, and this transformed our dynamics and helped us validate and love each other better. We were able to leave our two towers! We developed mutuality as justice and fairness began ruling our dynamics instead of codependent abdication on my part and domination on hers.

Healing took place in both of us as I took responsibility for my wounds, insecurities, and deficiencies, allowing God and Linda to love me to life. My confidence grew knowing that God loved me and was fathering me. It wasn't power I wanted, but intimacy.

Our confidence grew as we expressed our solid commitment to each other. I remember many times saying, in faith, "I know things feel awful right now, but I want you to know that I love you, am committed to you, and we're going to get through this. God's going to help us."

This gave her the strength to move forward in our transformation together.

We assured each other, "No one's going anywhere." In other words, "our castle is secure." We might have been bouncing off the ropes surrounding the ring, but we weren't going to abandon the contest. In the strength of our mutual commitment, I stopped fearing abandonment, which created inner courage.

I repented of going to her for approval and sought approval and validation from God instead, the true fountain of living water. The message I sent to her was, "I will be honest with you and engage with integrity instead of seeking your approval. I don't care if you disagree; I'm going to trust God and stand up for myself."

We created new habits and were freed from the slavery of old ones. It doesn't mean we don't need to be vigilant now, as we are always growing in marriage and old patterns are easy to fall back into. Any pattern can be transformed if we understand the cause and source and then invite God into it. He gives us wisdom when we ask for it. Find and deal with the cause, and the effect will go away.

Now we are going to explore how we can become more corporate by gaining a mentality that takes us out of considering just ourselves. We will examine some of the patterns that hold us back.

Chapter Seven

Break the Curse of "Me" over "We"

To one degree or another, most couples who are involved in a power struggle follow a similar pattern: they structure their lives so that true intimacy is virtually impossible
— Harville Hendrix

In the movie *The Family Man*, bachelor Jack Campbell is a high-powered playboy, a mover, and a shaker who suddenly finds himself living an alternate life in a small town with a wife and kids. When he concludes that this new life is here to stay, he tries to move his family to the city so he can recreate his self-serving life of success and power.

His wife, Kate, loves their home and life as it is, and is horrified at moving from the only house she's ever lived in, the house where she thought she and Jack would grow old and die. She is also terrified at the idea of taking their children from the only school and friends they've ever known.

Yet Kate finally reaches the place where she tells her husband, "If you really need this, Jack, if it's really that important to you, I'll do it. I love you and I choose us."[1]

I choose us.

These are the most powerful words a husband or wife can say to their beloved. The words themselves suggest a sacrifice, an act of submission that is made in love, a choice that is not without cost.

How Can You Become "Us"?

Becoming "us" is at the heart of everything. So why doesn't everyone do it? Why do many not experience it?

The answer is simple. It's hard to do and takes sacrifice.

Our self-serving nature—choosing "me" over "we"—is a menacing dragon standing in the way of the oneness we long for in our marriage. Slaying the dragon of selfishness and self-protection takes place when we "choose us."

We conquer this dragon when we lay down our selfishness and self-protection and choose "us" time and time again, in different settings and circumstances, in changing stages of life, and in our words and actions.

Now this dragon isn't easy to kill, since it doesn't look the same in every situation or marriage. It's made up of differing broken patterns, which means we might see this dragon reflected in a particular pattern, put it to rest, and then discover it in a different pattern. We will look at four of these.

"Choosing us" can be scary at first. I wasn't willing to yield much ground early on when Linda and I married. The first thing God did was start exposing me to my insecure defensiveness. I thought I had surrendered old hurts and wounds to God before I married Linda, but the real healing didn't begin until I risked loving again. I had to face and kill that dragon of defensiveness. This happened as I explored the fears behind my defensive reactions. I asked myself, *What am I trying to protect anyway? What am I so afraid of losing here? And What would happen if I did let my guard down?*

Let's look at these four ways the dragon of selfishness and self-protection can show up in our marriages, and how we can send it packing.

1. Healing Patterns of Power and Control

I will remember that my illusion of control is just that, an illusion.[2]

God doesn't "control" us. He gives us free will and lets us make choices. Think about Adam and Eve in the garden, the children of Israel in the wilderness, and all the family stories in the Bible; God never controlled anyone. Still, we can fall under the deception that we can use power to control our spouses and our marriages.

When husbands and wives try to control each other, they put their own needs and desires first. They are not thinking of the couple as an "us." Unity can't thrive or exist in an environment of control, because control doesn't appeal to the other's will, it takes over. This is why unity can only happen when the will is freely offered, not coerced or manipulated.

God doesn't enforce unity but commands a blessing upon it when we choose it (see Ps. 133). He blesses most the unity and agreement we find through honoring one another. There is no blessing in our continued fight over who has the wheel of control.

Control is typically rooted in fear, and selfishness is the energy that drives it. It is the opposite of love and respect. We fear that God or our spouse won't come through for us in ways we want or need them to, so we take things into our own hands. We do this by manipulating, which is our version of control. It's important to see its destructiveness and sinful roots and repent of it.

In our impatience and unwillingness to yield, we take hold of the wheel and attempt to *steer* our partner into dynamics that will meet our needs and give us what we want, even if it means degrading or invalidating them. We are playing God by engineering change through our fleshly means, instead of trusting God.

If we're honest, we're all familiar with ways to manipulate, and we've tasted the distance and loss of intimacy it creates. Consider these three truths:

1. It's impossible to manipulate your way into a happy marriage by trying to change your partner.
2. We must forsake control to experience love. We do this by repenting and turning from it. You could pray this:

Father, I see that I'm afraid and do not trust you. I

see that I'm controlling and manipulating my husband/wife. I repent of this and ask you to help me stop. Teach me to talk honestly about my needs and desires with my partner and let them respond.

3. The hallmark of a happy marriage isn't who is in charge or has the most power, but our ability to yield the power to each other.

2. Healing Patterns of Decision-Making

Another place the dragon of selfishness and self-protection can show up is in the realm of decision-making.

Our commitment to each other and our risk to trust and love will banish this dragon. A woman, feeling insecure in her husband's ability to make sound decisions, may withhold her vote of confidence or attempt decision-making without him. Perhaps he has some history of unwise choices. She may fear letting him lead because of how his potential poor judgment could affect her and the family. After all, they will all have to live with the consequences of their choices.

Her fear prevents her from following his leadership. There is a delicate balance here. Agreement, trust, and joint decision-making are what we want to grow into. He senses her reluctance to believe in him, feels pain, and emotionally withdraws into the tower, thinking, *Why doesn't she support me? She fights me on everything!*

He may think it's his fault and he's the problem, when in truth it's her fear creating the distance that is causing his pain. He just wants her to trust and believe in him. An insecure man may decide he knows what's best for the family and relegate her to a role of going along with his decisions. The playing field needs leveling. Then the couple can engage in a partnership that leads to agreement and mutual decision-making.

When he leaves her out this way, she feels devalued, unappreciated, and controlled. She will emotionally withdraw into her tower thinking, *Why doesn't he love or appreciate me, and value what I can offer? He doesn't even see or consider my needs at all. My voice needs to be counted for something.*

Instead of reaching an agreement together about important decisions, there is a power struggle, or no struggle at all as one dominates and does it all. Instead of open communication, there is manipulation, which is always done in the dark, outside of truth-telling. The struggle could be over finances, purchases, budgeting, rearing of children, discipline, or any of the stuff of life that requires decisions to be made and acted upon. Unpacking and honoring our fears and feelings takes the fire out of this dragon.

3. Healing Patterns of Emotional Honesty

The dragon of selfishness and self-protection also shows up in our fear of emotional honesty. This is due to the intensity of emotional pain. We have felt how emotional wounds can be more painful than physical ones and take longer to heal as well. When we've been hurt emotionally, it can be harder to open up until we feel safe.

If we have untreated wounds from our childhoods or past or current relationships, these wounds can shut us down and keep us from being emotionally honest with our spouses and ourselves. It causes us to self-protect, but not all self-protection is bad. We *need* to protect ourselves from unsafe people. But sometimes our efforts at self-protection are misplaced. Someone in the past hurt us deeply, and now we refuse to be emotionally vulnerable with anyone—including a spouse who loves us and longs for an emotionally safe and intimate marriage.

We were afraid to be emotionally honest when we first married. We both grew up in homes where transparency and safety weren't seen and had to overcome the fear of representing our true selves. The more wounds we've had in our past, the more self-protection we've built to survive. When we're in self-protection mode, we avoid emotional honesty and vulnerability because it isn't safe to share our real feelings. If you don't create safety for disclosure, you will sabotage the process when a conflict arises.

4. Healing Patterns of Fear of Conflict

Conflict and struggle are important elements in our metamorphosis as persons."[3]

Another way the dragon of selfishness and self-protection thrives is when we live in fear of conflict. Notice what gets in the way of "choosing us" isn't conflict but the *fear* of conflict. We fear it because it's uncomfortable, feels emotionally dangerous, and exposes us.

We mistakenly believe if we avoid conflict, we can safely live out our lives in a good enough shallow marriage, but one that can't meet our deeper needs for intimacy.

We shared earlier how conflict has a bad reputation. The truth is,

- There can be no mutuality without conflict.
- The discovery process that happens through conflict bonds us by knowing and being known.
- We need commitment to stay engaged without sabotaging the process.

As we gain talking skills, conflict becomes life-giving and hopeful as we feel connection and unity. We feel more connected than before the conflict ever happened. We experience the redemptive (healing) quality of conflict as our skills and practice help us connect.

Freedom through Truth-Telling

One of the greatest benefits of conflict is learning the truth about each other. We can love more deeply when we are operating in truthful relating. We choose to let our guards down and tell it like it is without game-playing or posturing. We can then respond from our true selves instead of hiding or lying. (This is our emotional intimacy promised land.)

We can only find this honest ground when we have secured the castle. We must walk here with tender, loving care and acceptance. Hearts cannot open without this.

During a recent conflict, Linda and I overcame our fear of talking about the wrong beliefs we had about each other. With this new understanding, we were able to honor one another's wounds and fears and be more sensitive in our approach and attitudes. Every time we understand more about our dynamics, it helps the next time we feel pain or fear.

The truth is, when we don't engage in conflict with emotional truth-telling, and a commitment to actively listen to each other, one of several things can happen:

- We can believe all sorts of lies about each other.
- We can project our insecurities onto our partners, adopting beliefs about how they feel that are false. We misread them.
- We won't receive love from our partners since all we perceive is judgment or disapproval from them.

On the other hand, conflict (or just everyday interaction) that invites honest questions and answers brings truth, and in truth there is safety. God and our spouse want to love us and hold us in our broken places. We choose to let them by coming out of hiding.

When writing and teaching on conflict, I talk about "dealing with the real." It means learning to talk with your spouse about what you are feeling and accepting those feelings. Broken relating can only be healed when it's talked about safely between the two of you. This can only happen when you engage in conflict and become truthful about what's going on in your heart.

Taking a Stand

When I take a stand, in my relationship with my wife Linda, it means I challenge the dynamics that are going on and call them out. I could say, "You didn't listen to a word I said and just rolled past me like my opinion meant nothing to you."

If she says, "So?"

Then I end the conversation and cease cooperating, saying, "Then we're done until you can respect me and treat me with dignity. Let me know when you're ready to try again."

In the early days, we had conversations like that. A counselor once told her she "needed to come off her high horse." I couldn't believe my ears as she agreed with him! The Lord used this counselor to say things I could never say and helped us both a lot. She needed to learn to honor me as her man. It didn't come easy, but we have grown together into mutually respecting friends who can extend honor and value equally to each other.

Boundaries empower you to move out of the victim role, become empowered, and fight for what is yours: respect and dignity.

You may ask, "What if my spouse disagrees or doesn't like what I say?" This is taken off the table when you stop fearing their response. This means when I feel dishonored or dismissed, I can challenge her with the rules of engagement. I can say, "We both agreed we weren't going to talk this way—let's take a time out, or let's try the active listening tool so we can hear each other and stop accusing and defending."

I can't cave into the anxiety of what she thinks or how she feels and remain silent. Dynamics change when abusive interaction is challenged. Remember, you have the power to regulate the conversation to make it respectful—or end it.

You need to be assertive with your opinion and value it equally alongside theirs. Not that it's superior, but it deserves equal consideration. Stick to your guns and call it out when it happens. Refuse to cooperate until they can respect and treat you with the dignity that belongs to you. We move into courage when we do and say healthy things in love without fearing what happens to the relationship.

I recall the days of early conflict in our marriage. When the power struggle would emerge, I would crumble and back down, having been conditioned by my upbringing.

I could practically hear the voice of my mother: *Don't you dare resist me!*

One time Linda said, "I can't believe how easily you cave in and back down."

This was because I was afraid to stand up for what I wanted or believed in. I didn't know how to be assertive, show up, and have it out in a healthy way. As I learned to represent myself and not fear rejection, our conflicts turned in a positive direction.

Don't Run Away

God is saying the words "I Love You," if only we could hear.
Even though he speaks the words, they can't get past our fear.
Because we know we're broken, we just can't let him in.
After all, his name is holy. *He can't look upon my sin.*

So we build a wall around our weakness, trying to hide it away,
Pretending it's not really there, or "I'll face it another day."
Lord, help me to embrace the parts broken deep inside,
To walk into your light of love and not to run and hide.

Jesus didn't say, "Try harder" but "Come and learn of me.
The way is not performance, but through grace and humility.
I know about your weaknesses better than you do.

Receive my love that makes you strong. My grace will see
you through."

—Daniel Lillyblad

CHAPTER EIGHT

Banish Shame

It is this blood, now in heaven before God for us, that is our bold-ness to enter in, even into the very Holiest of All.

— Andrew Murray

When someone is banished from a country, they've lost the right to be there. They've lost their citizenship and cannot return. Banishing shame means we recognize that it belongs to another kingdom and has no right to torment us any longer since we belong to the kingdom of God now. As citizens of God's kingdom, he banishes shame from our lives.

"Those who look to him are radiant; their faces are never covered with shame" (Ps. 34:5 NIV).

We will find that banishing shame involves not only our healing but also *closing the doors* on shame. Healing our hearts involves two players: what God does for us and what we do for ourselves. Our freedom from shame involves giving our hearts to Jesus. He then shows us where we have opened doors to shame and how to close them.

We close doors by identifying sinful access points that shame us. If someone has a besetting sin, the shame is stopped when the sin is confessed and renounced. God empowers us to close these doors. The doors don't go away; we must keep them closed. Shame cannot be banished if we open doors to let it back in. I like to say that when shame returns to knock on a door, Jesus opens it and says; *What are you doing here?*

We saw in chapter 3 how the enemy shames our identity to thwart our relationships. When we banish this shame and reclaim our whole identities as men and women, we can connect well sexually in marriage.

Our journey with God requires at times, painful surgery on our deep hearts. It takes the power of God the Father to remove the "leaven" of shame from our hearts, minds, and personalities. (Gal 5:9)

We need God's grace to penetrate our hearts as far as sin has— for us to know this healing. Sometimes this hurts as God visits our broken places to pour in his healing love. As Romans 5:20 tells us, "Where sin abounded, grace abounded much more." At times the healing of our deep wounds doesn't feel like grace, but through our faith, we can see and feel God's love. His powerful presence heals when we yield.

This journey takes our cooperation as prodigal pilgrims, returning to the Father's house. When shame consumes us, we've lost our way and have forgotten who we are. We've made poor choices and run to a far country. In a spiritual sense, we are all "prodigal sons" who have "come to our senses" and are on our way back to the Father's house. This means we have "left the pigpen" and are somewhere along the journey of homecoming. (Lk. 15:11-32)

Banishing Shame by Embracing an Accurate View of God

Good theology is important to fight our battles, resist the devil, and grow, but theology or head knowledge is not enough for transformation. We need relationships with the Father, Son, and Holy Spirit in an experiential way to heal and love in heartfelt, connecting ways.

The most important thing is not what our head knows but what our hearts know, and feel about God's love and grace. The Pharisees knew the Word (they memorized huge portions of the Torah), but they didn't know Jesus or the love of the Father. They resisted grace and opposed Jesus for not keeping the law and the rules.

Why is this important? Because it illustrates how you can know and quote the Bible and still live an untransformed life bound with chains of shame and legalism. It's about a relationship with Jesus, not being religious. It's not what we know but *who* we know.

How do you view God? As punisher or healer?

Reread these lines from the poem at the beginning of this chapter:

God is saying the words "I Love You," if only we could hear.

Even though he speaks the words, they can't get past our fear.
Because we know we're broken, we just can't let him in.
After all, his name is holy. He can't look upon my sin.

Why is it so hard to bring our broken places to God? Because of shame.

We're ashamed because we know we are broken and think there's nothing we can do about it. We feel helpless and disempowered, sometimes like victims.

We're afraid of our brokenness; we know it conquers us at times, and we feel shame. This shame causes us to retreat from ourselves and God.

It helps to know that our brokenness doesn't intimidate God. He's seen it all and has been healing broken hearts for a long time. We fear our out-of-control selves, and we fear God in a cringing way because we know we deserve punishment for our evil. Our heart response to him is fear because of our weakness within and the mocking voices of shame that accuse us.

You filthy thing, calls out the inner voice of shame. We expect from God the punishment which we think we deserve. When we heed the voice of shame, it robs our confidence and self-esteem. Yes, listening to lies shames us.

Adam in the Garden of Eden felt shame when Eve handed him the fruit and he ate it: "Then the eyes of both of them were opened, and they knew that they were naked, and they sewed fig leaves together and made themselves coverings" (Gen. 3:7).

They felt compelled to cover their genitals which were their expressions of sexual gender. "Their eyes were opened and they knew that they were naked." They hid the parts of themselves that distinguished them as male and female. The first thing they saw was that they had body parts their spouse didn't. There was no confusion there.

They experienced the equivalent of the devil pulling down their pants when they lost their innocence—they now felt shame. This is what he does: he captures our sexual identity (who we are as man or woman) through sin, then shames us for it, and sends us to our towers. At our core, we know something is wrong. And there is until Jesus comes and secures us.

So we hide from God and each other while doing penance to try to get back to God somehow. Our hope drains away as lies convince us we'll never be good enough no matter how hard we try. Our enemy tells us we must work our shame off before God as slaves before he will accept or love us. For Adam and Eve, the enemy stole their covering of innocence, which had been the glory of God, and gave them shame instead. We find God referring to this Genesis condition in the book of Revelation:

"I counsel you to buy from me gold refined by fire, so that you may be rich, and white garments so that you may clothe yourself and the shame of your nakedness may not be seen" (Rev. 3:18 ESV).

Simply put, shame keeps us from hearing and feeling the love of God. His words can't get past our fear. When God came after Adam, calling his name, Adam answered, "I heard Your voice in the garden, and I was afraid because I was naked, and I hid myself" (Gen. 3:10).

This is what shame does, it accuses us of our obvious nakedness and we run in fear from God. When we feel our shame and self-loathing, the last thing we want to hear is his voice. Because we know he's holy, his voice reminds us how sinful and different we are, and we fear the very voice that holds the healing words of love our hearts need.

"I heard Your voice . . . and I was afraid." So we hide. We fear God will reject us.

We think he'll punish our sin instead of healing it. We let shame rule and do its diabolical job by keeping our sins under wraps.

So we build a wall around our weakness, trying to hide it away, pretending it's not really there, or saying, *I'll face it another day.*

Only Jesus' loving mercy can crack the shame code that holds our hearts. He gives us boldness and confidence through his blood to come to the mercy seat where his transforming love awaits us. He calls us out of hiding and to come boldly into the Holiest of all through the blood of Jesus. (Heb. 4:14–16).

Banishing Shame by Renouncing Self-Hatred

Our need to hide our sin, expressed as the fig leaf in Genesis 3:7, is described by Andrew Comiskey in his book *Living Waters*:

> The leaf signifies our own tendency to try and hide from God and others. We feel shame, guilt, fear, and much pain due to our sexual and relational brokenness, yet we try and cover it up. For many, this cover-up results from

an ungodly shame. Pervasive feelings of being "bad" due to having certain kinds of difficulty comprise this shame. For some, this shame is rooted in childhood abuse—the poison of another's brokenness and perversion is taken in by the victim of the abuser's sin. (S)he internalizes the abuser's sin. (S)he in turn comes to view the self as bad and worthless, even deserving of such treatment.

Shame is also an issue for those with long-standing sexual struggles. Their persistence, often without respite, translates to the struggler: "It must be something about me. I must be bad." That deadening self-hatred and rejection are key symptoms of ungodly shame.

Before we proceed on, we must agree with the Father that His love for us is greater than our self-hatred and rejection. Due to that greater love, we can renounce self-hatred and rejection. We must learn to turn from the lie of ungodly shame and to turn to the truth of His love.[1]

Comiskey provides a suggested prayer for renouncing self-hatred:

Prayer of Renouncing Self-Hatred

"Father, we confess the sin of self-hatred. We confess we have turned against ourselves because of broken, out-of-control areas of our lives. We need your forgiveness for believing that our brokenness is more powerful than your love for us.

Establish us in your steadfast love. Burn off our shame with Your radiant presence."[2]

"Those who look to him are radiant; their faces are never covered with shame" (Psalm 34:5 NIV).

Banishing Shame through Self-Acceptance

Lord, help me to embrace the parts that are broken deep inside,
To walk into your light of love and not to run and hide.

The prayer for help to embrace our brokenness opens the door into our wounds with Jesus, a place we must go to heal. There we find courage, faith, and grace that empower us to face our broken selves without fear. We accept how broken we are and talk to Jesus about it. We learn to accept and hang out with who we really are. By inviting him into our brokenness, we allow him to help where we need it most, rather than hiding or denying help because of shame.

Self-acceptance brings me into the light of his love. There, with a spiritual mind, I receive grace and accept love and forgiveness. I resist the natural mind that tells me I'm unworthy and demands that I work. I bring to him in weakness that which I can do nothing about.

He says to us in essence, *Here's what's going on in here. This is what's broken, and this is what it's causing you to do. Let's work together to break these chains!*

When we bring our sin and weakness to him, we find grace, not by gritting our teeth working, but by resting in his presence. We transform when we are in his presence beholding him.

Wholeness and freedom are freely given through surrendering to his grace. We yield to his transforming power. It's important to remember we don't need to convince God to heal our hearts; he already wants to. He's waiting for our surrender so he can.

The self-applied balm of works for redemption can never remove shame, only increases it as we fail more on the performance path. In one of my first counseling sessions, a kind counselor said to me, "Dan, you need to lower the bar."

She knew by listening to me from my performance-oriented prison, that I was screwed down pretty tight. I knew much of the Bible but little of grace. My healing journey was just starting. I'd traveled the well-worn path of the religious zealot and had a lot of theology without healing of the heart. I needed to encounter the love and acceptance of the Father that I'd never known.

The problem with self-mastery is how it strives against grace and surrender. I thought I could obtain mastery through obedience. If I could just obey enough, my heart would heal, so I tried harder, became more disciplined, and learned more Bible. It doesn't work that way.

Our sinful pride, self-reliance, and self-determination make lowering the bar hard for us. When we are trying to please God through our works, it seems like a compromise to stop striving for acceptance. So we hide our broken places and cling to the false hope that we can master and conquer them. We cannot— A lifetime has a way of teaching this.

We tend to wall ourselves off when we deny our neediness and brokenness. We create a false self that's masked, while our true self remains broken and hidden, often addicted.

Leanne Payne calls this "the self-in-separation . . . and we all need the healings of the separations in our lives." She goes on to say, "The way shame manifests itself in our lives is varied, but the overall effect is basically the same. We end up cut off from ourselves, from others, and most importantly, from God the Father."[3]

Humble self-acceptance, not trying harder to conquer ourselves, is the pathway to healing. Only sitting in the healing presence of the Father's embrace brings the love and assurance our hearts need to heal. Healing comes to the brokenhearted, not the determined hard-hearted. As Psalm 51:17 says, "The sacrifices of God are a broken spirit, a broken and a contrite heart — these O God, You will not despise."

Nicholas Harnan writes, "This brokenness is what needs to be accepted. Unfortunately, this is what we tend to reject. Here the seeds of a corrosive self-hatred take root. This painful vulnerability is the characteristic feature of our humanity that most needs to be embraced in order to restore our human condition to a healed state."[4]

So, how do we find strength in weakness? It involves befriending and embracing the part of our heart that defeats us. This includes accepting our weakness, neediness, and vulnerability instead of despising it. We don't want to believe we are that vulnerable. Denying these broken places and walling them off keeps them out of the light and keeps us in hiding.

Brennan Manning says in *Abba's Child*, "Our skepticism and timidity keep us from belief and acceptance; however, we don't hate God, but we hate ourselves. Yet the spiritual life begins with the acceptance of our wounded self."[5]

We need to befriend our wounded selves and accept our broken parts. Only then can grace flow to those broken places. Jesus loves our broken hearts and every broken place. He wants to train us how to love and accept our hearts now, in the unhealed condition they are in. Only then can we let Grace in to do her healing work. As long as we're hating ourselves and who we are because of our sins, we can't access the grace of God. We can't hate ourselves and receive grace simultaneously. We need to allow the grace of God into our self-loathing.

Self-acceptance allows us to come out of hiding and walk into his light of love. This will banish shame, as shame can only live in the dark.

"He is found as we acknowledge and submit the broken and needy parts of ourselves to His greater love and order. He meets us there; He establishes His love and mercy to those areas we are most in need of Him."[6]

Banishing Shame by "Practicing His Presence"

Jesus didn't say, "Try harder" but "Come and learn of me.
The way is not performance but through grace and humility.
I know about your weaknesses better than you do.
Receive my love that makes you strong.
My grace will see you through."

As we've said, we will either practice his presence or practice works. It's easier to try to get it done than to let go and let God do it.

Jesus doesn't heal us by putting us to work. He heals us as we learn of his humility, tenderness, and desire to heal. He invites us to rest in him and enjoy his presence (Matt. 11:28).

This is the place where shame is burned away. This is where God frees us from the anxiety that our shame produces. He reveals where we are performing for his love and acceptance instead of surrendering to him.

But how do we surrender to his grace?

We stop doing and trying and start yielding and letting go. We cease our efforts to change things and wait for him. We gradually surrender, relax our hands that want control, and yield to receive from one greater than ourselves.

Brokenness and shame make it hard for us to receive the good or believe we are good. We know addiction and shame are not God's plan for us, but we don't know a way out, so we try to work to heal the disconnect and separation we feel within. Working harder can never heal the self in separation — our inner disconnects. Only the healing presence of the Father can.

He invites us into a relationship with Him, the Creator of our hearts, the only one who can heal the broken places.

As we listen in prayer he speaks the healing words that will transform what we believe about the Father.

You can pray this prayer before the Lord, and make it a part of your devotional life for its truth to take root in your heart.

Prayer of Affirmation of My Worth Before God

"Lord, I thank You that I am very special to you...that I am immeasurably precious to You...that you love me as though there were no one else to love . . . that it matters to you about me... that I am the apple of your eye . . . that your love for me is unconditional.

Thank you that You care about me so that you will never leave me or forsake me. Thank You that You understand my trouble as no one else does and will see me through this process of healing. I refuse to turn on myself any longer in obedience to Your love towards me.

I receive Your grace here in this particular area of my life, where it is most needed, and I will continue to extend grace here until I really believe that nothing can separate me from Your love. I refuse to reject myself because of this particular area of inadequacy or struggle.

May Your great love continue to free me from all expressions of self-hatred and rejection. Continue to release to me a hearty and holy self-acceptance."[7]

CHAPTER NINE
Heal Your Sexuality

*Thankfully, culture and habit do not determine true sexual ethics;
Jesus does. But what he asks of us, he enables us to realize. His
blood makes us his own, and his Spirit fills us with power from on
high, confirming whose we are and what we are for.*

— Andrew Comiskey

When we talk about healing our sexuality, it's about finding freedom and staying free from sexual bondage, no matter
where we've been sexually. This is a lifetime healing journey
that won't be completed when we turn the next few pages,
but we will have begun the quest. We will have an awareness
of ourselves and a strategy for victory — which will include
bringing our sexual history before God — seeking repentance,
deliverance, and freedom in Christ.

For each of us, our sexual engagement once married is strongly influenced by how we've behaved sexually in the past, and the sexual messages or experiences we've been exposed to; willingly or unwillingly.

I know this can be a painful subject and hard to face, and many of us possess histories that carry shame and regret. We have wounded others sexually and suffered abuse and wounds ourselves. "To be set free for real love, we must face our need for love in historic areas of neglect or hurt."[1]

We need this discussion to bring these wounds into the context of God's love and mercy for healing if we are ever to banish stubborn habits in our sexual expression. Sexual brokenness hinders our sexual oneness, while a whole and healthy sexual connection supports a strong marriage.

I found a verse from the Message translation of the Bible that says it well:

> You know the guidelines we laid out for you from the Master Jesus. God wants you to live a pure life. Keep yourselves from sexual promiscuity. Learn to appreciate and give dignity to your body, not abusing it, as is so common to those who know nothing of God. . . . God hasn't invited us into a disorderly, grungy life but into something beautiful — as beautiful on the inside as the outside (1 Thess. 4:3–7).

We live in a world with low standards and strong sexual influences, and we need a powerful truth to break free from the world's chains and live sexually pure for God, our spouses, and our families.

It's easy to get trapped in sexual prisons in or out of marriage, but escaping them is difficult. In the next two chapters, we reveal a strategy to get free and stay free sexually. We'll learn how to protect our marriages by showing how to put out all strange fires and come under God's empowering protection.

Our First Step—Our Call to Consecration

"For this is the will of God, your sanctification: that you should abstain from sexual immorality; that each of you should know how to possess his own vessel in sanctification and honor, not in the passion of lust, like the Gentiles who do not know God" (1 Thess. 4:3-5).

According to *Roget's Thesaurus*, sanctification is "the action or process of being freed from sin or purified."

This is seen in Scripture as a process in which we are joined to Jesus as our sanctifier. (Heb. 2:11-15; 10:14). I call it a healing journey. On this journey, we are empowered by our savior and redeemer Jesus, who has defeated the devil and his enslaving influences over our souls. Through our union with him, all we need is supplied to us by faith, through the power of his Holy Spirit to live for him and walk in purity.

Here's our dilemma: We've given parts of our hearts away, and we need to get them back. We've built false altars of worship and burned incense there, giving away our emotions and attention.

This sexual yielding, or idolatry, often has been at the expense of our lovers and our families and has cost us our freedom. It is far more than a weak area, habit, or addiction. We are captives in a foreign land, far away from the kingdom of God. We've got to recover our hearts and return to our promised land.

Our sexuality needs a healing journey, which starts when our sex is yielded over to God. When our sexuality is out of control or controls us, it needs to be consecrated to God to be corralled.

The language of consecration to God says, "I am Yours, You are mine. There are no others besides You." Sound familiar? It's our wedding vows to God.

To consecrate, according to *Roget's Thesaurus*, means "to yield to authority or to empower." When we marry our spouses and enter into a covenant with them — we are consecrating ourselves to each other. We exchange vows and rings as our symbol of faithfulness, integrity, and fidelity. When we marry, we are yielding authority over our bodies to our spouses. We consecrate our bodies to them. I Corinthians 7:4 reveals this: "The wife does not have authority over her own body, but the husband does. And likewise, the husband does not have authority over his own body, but the wife does."

Although this was written in the context of not withholding sex from one another, it's also in the context of the husband and wife giving up the right to use their sexuality in any other way than making love to their spouse. The married spouse no longer has the authority to use their sex outside of the marriage covenant.

We yield authority over our bodies in marriage and consecrate ourselves to God. We surrender control of how we use sex and yield our sexuality to him. We settle the question of who we belong to sexually with finality. We make our *Consecration Statement* by saying

> *God has authority over the sexual arena of my life and is empowering me to live sexually for him with integrity and honor. This is the only way I will use my sexuality. I make myself unavailable to any other sexual expressions outside of God's will. That's not who I am and that's not what my body is for — my body is for the Lord.* (1 Cor. 6:13)

By doing this — orienting and aligning ourselves against sin and sexual immorality, we gain authority over our sexual impulses. We give Jesus lordship, and our desires are Holy Spirit- empowered to be used only for him. This means making God-honoring sexual choices in our thoughts and deeds that lead us to sexual purity in life whether single or married.

Without making this consecration statement and living it out with whole sexual expression, we cannot stand against the immoral tide of the culture we live in daily. We will be overcome without a solid consecration to Jesus. With this commitment, we can resist the devil, and he will flee from us. Our consecration, in essence, removes us from the devil's influence in our sexual arena. Our life now exists outside his control over our sexuality — as we resist him (James 4:7).

This is an ongoing walk and growth into sexual maturity and discipline. It is a situational and progressive yielding to Jesus of our sexual choices as we grow with him. Adolescent sexuality is out of control, (regardless of your age). Adult sexuality puts away childish sex outside of the covenant and grows into discipline, fidelity, and faithfulness. This is what covenant means. It doesn't mean we walk on water in our thought life.

It does mean we can live free from mental torment with sexual thoughts, or sexual bondage, trapped in an immoral lifestyle or addiction (Eph. 4:17-24).

Think of consecrating yourself as making God your sexual guidance or navigation system. We get lost without it, lose our coordinates, and our sex goes off course. We are then chained to dark places and habits. Because of Jesus, we have hope we can move from off-course sexuality and make Jesus our destination station.

The devil is the enforcer of unconsecrated sex and makes sure that unguided sex will lead to bondage. When we don't yield our sex to God, the devil gladly takes over. When we lose our consecration, we become morally impure and lose "authority" over our sex drive, having yielded it to another "master," (Rom. 6:16).

What we yield to Jesus becomes empowered for use in freedom. What we yield to the devil is empowered for use in slavery.

C.S. Lewis writes in The Screwtape Letters—One demon training another how to deceive humans says — *Everything has to be twisted before it's any use to us.*[2]

My experience is the devil pays close attention to what we are doing with our sexuality to seduce us onto dark paths. He looks for an opportune time, seeking to devour (1 Pet. 5:8). We are especially vulnerable to temptation when things aren't going well at home, or there is sexual struggle or lack of connecting between spouses—for whatever reason. The importance of consecration to stay out of the devil's grip sexually cannot be overstated.

Mercy Triumphs Over Judgment

While Jesus declares a high moral standard, he shows mercy and grace to sinners and strugglers alike. He doesn't set a standard we can't reach and then shame or condemn us when we fail.

His encounters with broken ones on earth were reliably the same; merciful and grace-filled. There was the woman caught in adultery, in the very act. Jesus defended her against her accusers and raised the standard for mercy. He wouldn't allow the keepers of the law to kill her. He pardoned her with the words, "Neither do I condemn you; go and sin no more" (John 8:11). She didn't know that morning that her sin would bring her face to face with Jesus — that He would deliver her off death row and forgive her with a new beginning. This brings hope to us in our struggles.

Then there's the Samaritan woman at the well.

When Jesus revealed to her that he was the Messiah and she asked for the living water, he said, "Go get your husband" (John 4:16 ERV).

He was meeting her in the arena of relational and sexual brokenness, where she had failed and was failing in her marriages. She found that her relational failures didn't disqualify her but, rather, drew Jesus to her.

He sought her out, on assignment, knowing she'd been married five times and was living with a man who wasn't her husband, and according to John 4:4, Jesus "had to go through the country of Samaria." The Father sent Jesus to her, this relational failure who was living in sin. The Father also sends him to us.

My point is this: He meets us where we live and offers hope, mercy, and redemption in the middle of our broken real-life realities. He never shouts judgment, pours out condemnation, or mocks us through the walls of our self-made prisons.

Rather, He seeks us out in our struggles and places of bondage, to connect with us where we are broken inside, and heals us. Jesus explains, "Those who are well have no need of a physician, but those who are sick. I have not come to call the righteous, but sinners, to repentance" (Luke 5:31–32).

Jesus is drawn to our needs and wants to spend time with us, knowing we need his healing and help in our hearts. We are the sick ones needing a physician, Christian or not. "Getting saved" doesn't remove your sexual brokenness or close all your sin doors. Maintaining our covenant relationship with him throughout our entire lives, and yielding to his sanctification process heals our sexual brokenness, and *keeps us free* so we can live for him.

He came to heal the brokenhearted and set the captives free, but we can't expect him to do it all (Isaiah 61:1). We have a responsibility, to do our part, and work with him. As we walk with Jesus, he teaches us to yield to him and follow his strategy to tear down the high places of sexual immorality. We are called to walk worthy of his calling (Eph. 4:1).

How God Sees Us

From God's perspective, he sees that we've given parts of our hearts away and need help getting them back. He sees us as lost sheep, bound in shackles, needing freedom, not filthy sinners who need judgment. Jesus said, "I didn't come to judge the world but to save the world" (John 12:47).

He has come for our hearts. He sees this broken sexual part of our hearts as lost. He wants to recover our hearts and desires—but we have to want freedom. Our will has been weakened by sin, and Jesus has come to empower this will to choose life and live again for Him. He has the power and gives us the courage and confidence to get our hearts and our sex back for Him.

Where Many of Us Are

Though seldom taught or discussed outside recovery books, when we marry, we bring the products of our worldly, sexually charged history into the marriage bed. We carry in sexual backpacks containing our wounds and trauma that we need help unpacking. Left unaddressed, our sexual intimacy and enjoyment with our spouse are hindered.

How your sexual history impacts your marriage depends on family dysfunction, your generational inheritance, and the relationships or abuse you've known. Our attitudes toward sex—the things we've viewed, and the habits we've developed—are born of our history and are often not good for married life. Broken sexual patterns tagging along with us can steal mutual intimacy and defile our marriage bed. Any sexual expressions outside those with our spouse defile and disconnect us.

Sexual intimacy is often stolen after marriage through sexual brokenness, unfaithfulness, and addictions. Sexual energy escaping a marriage in any form is like a slow leak in a tire that will go flat without repair. The energy intended to be used for the couple is dissipated and weakened by one or both if sexual energy escapes the marriage.

These illicit actions—fantasized or acted out with others, become sexual addictions in both men and women. This is called false intimacy, and it is cheating on our spouses.

In marriage, if I fantasize or act out sexually, (sex with another partner), I am cheating on my spouse because what I promised to her, (my exclusive sex when I entered a covenant with her and God), I am giving away to another. Each time I do, it's easier the next time. If I continue, my desire for another experience increases, and the chain is forged.

These are the altars of idolatry, or high places we've built throughout our lives to help us cope with the stress and pain of living. When we seek illicit sexual pleasure, we find false emotional validation or feelings of belonging or being loved. It is an empty imitation, a powerful illusion. This is known as false intimacy.

We built these altars to survive and cope, but they may remain now in marriage with our hearts still connected to them ready to do damage. Scripture warns us, "Marriage should be honored by all, and the marriage bed kept pure, for

God will judge the adulterer and all the sexually immoral" (Heb. 13:4 NIV).

WWJD?—The Jesus Standard

Remember the rubber wristbands with those initials on them—WWJD? We wore them as a reminder to ask ourselves, "What would Jesus do?"

How would he have responded in attitude, words, and actions? How can I honor him as a follower now? What about Jesus and sex?

One area he cleared up was the standard he set for our sexuality. He stated how he felt about our sexual thought lives and what our eyes watch.

"You have heard that it was said of old, 'You shall not commit adultery.' But I say to you that whoever looks at a woman to lust for her has already committed adultery with her in his heart" (Matt. 5:27–28).

In one sentence, he brought a new revelation about how God sees things. Followers could not get away with a deceptive belief that says, *I can look all I want and as long as I'm not touching, I'm not sinning.* He knows how strongholds in the mind and heart can create the same connections as when you are physically having sex with another. Jesus called fantasy lust for what it is, stealing what doesn't belong to you. He is now saying, *You don't have to go to bed with someone to commit the act in your heart. As far as I'm concerned, if you are doing it in your mind, it's the same to me as if you slept with them — it is a sin.*

Our imaginations and minds are powerful and sought by both God and the devil (2 Cor. 4:4; 2 Cor. 10:5; Eph. 4:17–24).

Our Maker knows the creative power of the imagination when it's under enemy control. We can easily trade the real for an illusion and embrace the lies of false intimacy as no big deal. Of course, acting it out, having sex with another than our spouse, is worse—but our hearts are still sinning if we allow fantasy lust thoughts to control our sexual emotions and actions. The point is that Jesus is raising the bar. This is his standard and we are morally obligated to seek to live it out if we say we are his followers. We need a moral edge to constrain us or we are just like the world and lack power and live a false witness.

Objectifying others—i.e., making them the target of our lustful eyes—uses and degrades them selfishly and opposes love. Both sexes do this, and temptation to lust is common to all (1 Cor. 10:11–14; James 1:13–15).

After saying lusting with the eyes is as bad as the act, Jesus then talks about plucking out eyes or cutting off hands that cause us to lust, so our whole body isn't cast into hell. This shows that radical steps are needed to live up to this raised standard of morality Jesus is teaching. We know he doesn't want us to remove body parts, but he does want us to take the steps needed to find freedom— amputating as it were, idolatrous parts of ourselves in our hearts that are serving sin. Nothing will change without this circumcision of the heart.

He wants to help us consecrate our sexuality and constrain our sexual desire for him and our spouses. He wants to help us pull down the high places in our hearts.

I love the scene in the movie *The Family Man* where Nicholas Cage is contemplating an affair. He boasts, "The rules don't apply to me," and asks his best friend for the woman's phone number. His friend can't believe what he's hearing and is admonishing him about being unfaithful. He is angry that Jack Campbell would so easily destroy everything he has, betray his family, and break the heart of his beautiful wife. He says, "The bank of fidelity is a tough customer. You make a withdrawal somewhere else, and they close your account! Forever!"[3]

Research confirms that men and women alike, Christian or not, foreclose on their fidelity accounts often, if not in their actions then in their minds. Maybe they haven't cheated on their partner physically, but they are escaping into fantasy sex through different mediums. This fantasy realm is where strongholds, imaginations, and idols in the mind are formed and need to be torn down (2 Cor. 10:5). Strongholds are false patterns of thinking—lies that rule what we believe and are not connected to truth. The devil told Eve before she ate the apple, *You won't surely die.*

Before we come to Jesus we have unrenewed minds that resist God. Romans 8:5–8 teaches us that we have a mind of the flesh or a carnal mind that can cause us to "set our minds on the things of the flesh." We then "live according to the flesh," and are unable to walk a spiritual life.

The carnal mind rebels against God and cannot submit to his kingdom's values. "For to be carnally minded is death, but to be spiritually minded is life and peace" (Rom. 8:6). The belief systems that control us are the strongholds that need to be transformed so we can live in the spirit and please God.

Hope for the Past and the Future

How do you relate to your husband or wife sexually? Is guilt or shame from your past getting in the way? Your relationship with your past and how you feel about it can connect you intimately with your partner or create barriers between you.

I want to talk now about sinful things we've experienced in our past and how we feel about them now. God uses us even after a life of not serving him and living a life of sin against him. We can have a redemptive life after failure if we put our trust in him. We are not debilitated by sinful pasts, rather God uses us in redemptive ways *because* of our pasts. He turns our past sins and weaknesses into areas that are used for his glory.

There are many characters in the Bible with difficult pasts that contain regrettable things they did. They needed to overcome their mistakes and trust God for forgiveness to deliver them from shame. King David, the psalmist of Israel and a man after God's own heart, had some things to live down. There were self-made consequences he had to live with and forgive himself for. Psalm 51, which he wrote *after* he went into Bathsheba and killed her husband, Uriah, is a reflection on this.

David's redemption story illustrates that our past doesn't define our future and our sin and brokenness are common to man. Our past is no problem for God to clean up. Old things are passing away, and all things are becoming new (2 Cor. 5:17). We have a new identity now and are not who we were, no matter what past we carry with us.

Accepting and Forgiving Our Past

Nothing the devil has done to us sexually or to our hearts can separate us from God's love. Through faith, our hearts can live fully and freely because of Jesus' healing work of restoration.

God wants us to forgive ourselves for everything we ever did in our past. Everything? Yes, everything. I've found the journey of self-forgiveness to be emotionally liberating. Shame and guilt can still echo from the past into our present. If I can forgive myself as God has it ceases to bind me. When a past shameful thing comes to mind, I can say, *God has forgiven me, and I forgive myself for the choices I made in that situation. I accept who I was then, and thank Jesus he has made me into a new person. I accept my past as part of my story and thank God that He is writing a new one for me. I put on Your robe of righteousness and accept Your atoning blood for cleansing.*

Making this declaration every time past thoughts, events, or brokenness come up, bars the door to shame or degradation that can come through memory of past things. I can say, *Thank you, Jesus – that is under the blood – and I am free from it.*

Doing this relieves the anxiety I feel to undo the past or try to redeem myself in some way. I can't undo what I've done or who I've been; I leave all that to Jesus and the cross and his work to make me new.

Forgiving myself helps me believe he has forgiven and redeemed my past. This enables me to live comfortably with it without guilt, shame, or anxiety.

The cross intercepts the oppression of my past and I am freed from it. When shame tries to whisper to me I remind the devil of what Jesus did for me on the cross, what his blood did to cleanse me and to defeat him. Things get quiet after that.

Jesus settled the debt so I don't have to pay it and now wants me to forgive myself as deeply as he has. Believing this is part of the healing process for my heart.

He wants to give us hope for our past and faith that he's using it for redemptive purposes. It's easy to keep carrying shame when we aren't yet reconciled to our past and who we were.

When we accept our past selves, that broken image can be healed. When we change our attitude to who we were before—our younger, sinful selves—we will be kinder to ourselves. Remember the line from the poem in the last chapter: *Lord, help me to embrace the parts broken deep inside.* Instead of pushing the *broken me* away from the light, I bring him *into* the light. I accept and forgive him, as God has.

Yes, you did those things, but God forgave you, and now you must forgive yourself. Forgive yourself for the poor choices that caused so much shipwreck and pain. Punishing ourselves for the past only torments us emotionally. Forgive *who you were* instead of locking that person away behind some door in a basement vault, where you can hear them rattling around. You can't make your former self pay the price. Jesus doesn't. He paid the price.

Yes, accept the present your past created. You can find life now, enjoying God's power of redemption every day, or you will live in regret, pining for *what could have been if only I hadn't* . . . Self-forgiveness breaks the depression you carry by *not* forgiving yourself.

Humility frees us from trying to pay the debt Jesus paid on the cross. Receive his gift of forgiveness of our past, present, and future.

Forgiving Is Not Forgetting

God forgives our past; he doesn't erase it, and it doesn't cease to exist. He heals our memories and breaks their power to shame and control us, but it doesn't mean you *can't remember.* At times, when something comes to mind, it could be the Holy Spirit bringing the memory so he can heal where shame is still lurking. God doesn't erase our minds; our memories are part of who we are. He renews our minds and transforms them (Rom. 12:1–2).

We must forgive our pasts, hold our heads high, let Jesus speak through our story, and let his blood speak for us (Heb. 12:24). We know that the devil, king of shame, remembers our past and wants us to hate our younger selves, continue to identify with those earlier versions of ourselves, and feel shame now. The devil is called the accuser of the brethren, and Jesus has cast him down (Rev. 12:10–11).

Forgiving myself helps Jesus access the broken me. My past is part of the broken me, who's growing in transformation and moving from glory to glory (2 Cor. 3:18). Jesus accepts our past as part of what makes us who we are. He's redeeming it in our lives every day.

I think we can make our brokenness bigger than God by making such a big deal out of it. Think how many sin-ravaged hearts God has seen and redeemed. It's the devil's lie to think ours is unique and unsavable and we are beyond hope and out of God's reach. *Jesus is not enough* — is the devil's mind game. Your faith in Jesus shuts him up. *Jesus is enough.* "And you are complete in Him, who is the head of all principality and power" (Col. 2:10).

We grow spiritually when we learn to live with our past since it is always going to be part of who we are and declares our story.

God can and does leverage our broken past for a whole future free of guilt and shame. So we choose to accept our past and forgive ourselves for it and all the choices we've made. We determine we'll no longer live in regret or beat ourselves up. We renounce the shame that steals our joy and hope. "Let the redeemed of the LORD say so, whom He has redeemed from the hand of the enemy" (Ps. 107:2).

Prayer of Self-Forgiveness (read aloud)

> *Thank you, Lord, for your forgiveness and mercy. I choose now to extend grace to myself, and I forgive myself for my past. I forgive the younger me who made so many mistakes and poor choices. I forgive myself for the heartache and pain I caused for myself and many others.*
>
> *I forgive myself for the poor choices that created part of the life I live now. I forgive myself for the consequences of bad choices and mistakes made. I choose to no longer punish myself or listen to echoes of shame from my past. Thank you for a full redemption, Jesus.*

"In Him we have redemption through His blood, the forgiveness of sins, according to the riches of His grace" (Eph. 1:7).

CHAPTER TEN
Escape from Idolatry

If our eyes were fully open to the reality of the spiritual world and we understood the consequences of sinning against our own bodies, we would obey Scripture and flee from sexual immorality.
— Neil T. Anderson

Doors and High Places

The next step to gaining our freedom is to close doors that steal sexual intimacy in marriage. We lose this intimacy through sexual idolatry. Our desire and attention get hijacked through broken sexuality. The sex designed to connect a marriage through a whole sexual union is stolen and given to another.

To close a door means to stop the sexual sin in our lives that allows access to the demonic influence of sexual sin and idolatry. We will define and show how to remove the high places — altars of idolatry we've built along the way that remain in our lives and bind us to sexual sin.

Closing doors means stopping whatever sexual sin you are doing, repenting, and setting your will against it. Access is denied. To say one has doors still opened, means they are still walking in immorality as defined in the Bible. They haven't given their sexuality to God but are still engaging in sexually immoral acts, and are slaves to sin (Rom. 6:16).

Never in biblical history did God give his people the right to make up the rules regarding sexuality or morality. This was Adam and Eve's problem. They tried to change the rules and *be like God,* setting their own boundaries for morality (Gen. 3:4-6). God declared his worship boundaries for his followers in the first commandment when he said

> You shall have no other gods before me — You shall not bow down to them or serve them. For I the Lord your God, am a jealous God, visiting the iniquity of the fathers upon the children to the third and fourth generations of those who hate me. (Exodus 20:3, 5)

These verses indicate that sin and its consequences are handed down from one generation up to the third and fourth following. This sustains the belief that generational strongholds are passed down through opened doors of sin. These cycles of bondage will continue until someone in the generational line stands up and says, "Stop! That's enough. No more. It stops here."

Sexual sin was seen in King David's life, who repented of it (Ps. 51), but then sexual sin was lived out exponentially in his son King Solomon's life. Even though God warned Solomon, his heart was hardened through sexual sin (1 Kings 11:1-13). He made treaties with foreign nations, married their women, worshipped their gods, and built high places.

In Exodus 20, God says *we hate him* if we bow down at these altars, and states that he will visit the iniquity of the fathers upon the generations following us with our sin. Where do we stand in *our* generational line?

Repenting, renouncing our idols, and returning to God for mercy is the only way to close doors on the devil, find freedom, rule our spirits, and possess our vessels (1 Thess. 4:4).

We can't break spiritual laws without consequences. Yes God forgives, but we can stay enslaved to sexual sin by continuing in it with open doors. In this condition, the devil has access to our spirits. We are vulnerable while rendered powerless in our spiritual lives with our walls down. We can be reduced to a crust of bread while our precious life is preyed upon (Pr. 6:26).

Remember, when we give our sexuality to God, he empowers it to be used for him. Whatever we yield to the devil becomes twisted — empowered by him through attachment — to be used destructively in relationships. We'll show prayers of repenting and renouncing at the end of this chapter to demonstrate the language needed to close these doors.

In biblical times, the altars found at the demonic high places were constructed of wood, stone, or metal. Obscene sexual images were present, and specific gods and goddesses were worshipped there by having sex with the temple prostitutes — priests and priestesses dedicated to that god.

The high places of idolatry today don't look the same, and the gods worshipped there aren't as obvious, but the same perversion is worked out at other modern altars: such as strip joints, brothels, parlors, or at a computer terminal, digital device, TV or theater. Wherever sexual immorality is practiced, doors are opened to the demonic as incense is offered up to the gods of broken sexuality. This incense is the giving away of heart and emotion in worship to the gods of broken sex. Bondage always results.

Identify the Sexuality Myths Hurting Your Marriage

Many have naïve beliefs and false expectations about their sexuality and marriage. These ways of thinking can leave new lovers unprepared for the sexual struggles they will face.

Most are unaware of the sexual homework awaiting them in their new marriage, thinking marriage will heal them sexually by providing a sexual outlet. But it doesn't undo our brokenness. Before marrying, many have opened doors that lead to addictive strongholds of idolatry. These strongholds don't fade away or loosen their grip until confronted spiritually.

Why do we need to talk about this? Because marriage is under attack. We live in the world's sexual standard of living that flows downstream towards immorality. Talking about it equips us to fight the good fight of faith live clean—to guard our hearts.

Following are some myths about marriage that leave us unprepared after we say, "I do." Before diving into these, I want to acknowledge that all of us are different and no two backgrounds or histories are the same. Addressing addiction and sexual brokenness doesn't mean every reader will struggle at some of the levels described. The determining factor will be whether one's sexuality is submitted to Christ or not.

You may be fortunate enough to live in or come from a Christian home with a stable family and less dysfunction. You will likely have less sexual brokenness to reckon with. This language may seem foreign to you. Others less fortunate, having more dysfunction, trauma, and abuse in their story, will relate clearly and find help in this narrative. Many strugglers will find freedom from longtime chains that have held them captive. This is my prayer and motivation for writing these last two chapters.

Myth: Holy matrimony will transform me.

This myth says, *When we marry, the sexual struggles I've had with addiction or unfaithfulness in relationships will go away once I'm married.*

Those believing this myth don't understand how our sexuality works. The sexual person you were before you married is who you are now, except now you are sporting a wedding band.

Who you are sexually crosses the threshold with you. The level of personal victory you have achieved over your sexuality and temptation is what you enter with — it doesn't change. We bring our sexual addictions and fantasy lives into marriage. The marriage myth says that *the broken person you were before marriage no longer exists after marriage* — as if marriage is a magic wand that breaks the spell of sexual bondage. This isn't how it works. If you view pornography and have an active sexual fantasy life before marriage, those entrenched sexual habits and ways of thinking don't cease because you're married now.

Fantasy unions made in the mind whether you are male or female aren't broken by marriage. In many cases, the new spouse is just added to the fantasy harem. This isn't confined to pictures on a page or screen. Novels can also provide an escape from reality and steal the reader's heart from the marriage as they fantasize about what it would be like to be with that lover. Those who use sex this way remain connected to their fantasy lovers until these soul ties are broken, and the engagement in fantasy is stopped, which closes the door.

Using pornography or reading racy novels keeps fantasy lovers alive and well, available for use on the stage of your imagination whenever you call them up. This happens more and more often as addiction tightens its grip and claims your heart — leaving your spouse with less and less of it. Notice it's the activity of using, looking, and reading, that keeps the door open.

I'm not saying this person doesn't love their spouse, it's just that they can't love them with their whole heart. They can only offer the parts that aren't captured by addiction and given to another. We can't love God and idols — we can't love our spouses and idols—not with the little foxes spoiling the vine (Song 2:15).

Early History

Our sex tends to get stuck where it first started. This means sexual habits developed early in life — when we are first aware of our sex and become sexually active—will keep us bound there emotionally and sexually until we address and grow out of these habits. At first, we may not know what's normal or what that even looks like. There are often no supportive parents or godly mentors to tell us or help us, especially in the vulnerable years of our emerging sexuality.

Sadly, with so many broken homes and single-parent families, the child is left without a father figure. Even if a father figure is there, they often teach children to perform and keep rules but don't know how to care for their hearts and enter into life's struggles with them.

Let's say an adolescent becomes addicted to pornography or develops a promiscuous lifestyle. He or she will continue to be stuck, or addicted until action is taken to change that sexual lifestyle. Many young men never grow out of the adolescent stage of sexuality—in which they are sexually obsessed—and are trained to use and exploit women. These are womanizers who use women's bodies for sex but won't commit to them. Young ladies also need Dad to be there for them, valuing and affirming their femininity, covering and protecting their vulnerable hearts. Then they are secured in Dad's love, so they don't look for that love in broken places as their sexuality emerges.

Broken sexual patterns that emerge early in life define where we start on our sexual journey. Until we surrender to God, repent, consecrate ourselves, and turn from our idols, we stay stuck in these broken sexual lifestyles. We may want to stop but can't, with limited success because of idolatry's chains. They are spiritual chains and we need help. They require a spiritual authority to break.

If marriage did the trick of freeing us sexually to be faithful, everyone would have responsible sexuality from the wedding on. We all know this isn't the case, and many marrieds continue in irresponsible sexual behavior even after tying the knot.

I recently talked to a young woman waiting tables who just divorced because her husband slept with her best girl-friend. I'm sure he meant well when he married her. What happened? The two refrains I hear most are, *They cheated on me,* or *We just grew apart.*

Marriage is simply not a strong enough cage to contain unsubmitted sexuality — one not being managed by the power of God. Matrimony is "holy" only when the two partners make it holy by living sexually pure before God and one another, in thought and deed.

This is a growth process as the Lord shows us the strong-holds that remain in our lives to be purged by him. He sustains us with his grace and tenderly exposes our brokenness for healing. He then gives us spiritual strategies to defeat the snares that would trap us.

Myth: This should be easy. I don't need to fight the holy war for the marriage I want.

I thought when I married Linda, it would be easier than it was. I supposed that sexual temptations would cease, and we would merge into blissful oneness. After all, I had read so many books, had been preparing, and stayed faithful to God and myself. My struggles to keep my mind pure would leave because I thought, *I'd left all that behind me.* Being married would be the magic bullet for all that. I expected more freedom from married life and was surprised by the ongoing struggles I faced. My new married status wasn't freeing me from temptation and I needed more work than just coasting into marriage.

Oh, I said I loved Jesus, and my wife, but my heart wasn't free to love her and God wholeheartedly. I was also in love with some other things that were getting in the way. The temple, my body, and my mind needed cleansing, and I was humbled by the work still needing to be done.

Myth: Go ahead, it's fine; everyone else does it!

In my mental battles with sexual temptation, I've seen how the devil bombards me with thoughts and visual images to weaken my resolve. It's not that there's sex on the mind all the time, but there are times when the devil seeks to break me down with snares and traps (2 Cor. 2:11).

He launches an offensive so you will bow down to him. He seeks "an opportune time" (Luke 4:13), as he did with Jesus when he offered all his kingdoms if Jesus would only "bow down and worship" him (Matt. 4:9 NIV). There are times when we must actively resist him, out loud.

Once, I was driving into town for work, and there was a larger-than-life billboard with an enchanting large-breasted woman hanging out of a skimpy top. She was leaving little to the imagination, as she smiled with arms open and invited me to herself.

She was the advertising activator for the topless bar. The message next to her on the billboard was, "Go ahead, everyone else is!"

The subliminal message was, *Come and bow down to me. Come and join the other sex slaves in my jail of sexual lust and addiction. Everyone else is, no reason for you to be left out in the cold. Come in for some goddess worship.*

My heart rate went up. Was it God's presence there to protect me or was my body responding? It reminded me of Galadriel in *The Lord of the Rings* when she took the ring from Frodo and manifested into the demonic goddess until she resisted temptation and passed her test.

Deal with Temptation

Even though the woman on the billboard was beautiful, my response was not lust but anger. I felt degraded by the devil's boldness as he mocked my vulnerability to put me to shame. My emotional response was indignation. *How dare you!*

Don't say — It's just porn, or it's just a billboard. No! It's demonic, and a powerful tool of bondage the devil uses against men and women alike. Don't be deceived by the lie like Adam and Eve when the devil told them — *You will not surely die* (Gen. 3:4).

Part of spiritual warfare and our battle with the shame game is sexual temptation. It's important to note that being tempted doesn't defile you, but giving in to lust and giving birth to sin is where shame and death are introduced (James 1:13–15).

We can choose to push the devil back and resist him. Sexual attacks are assaults on our identity — who we are sexually, and the devil's attempt to shame us. We can defeat him when we take charge of our will and our desire and resist him. We possess that authority. It's been said, "It's not a sin if a bird flies over — it becomes a sin when you let it build a nest in your hair."

It's not a sin when the devil tempts us, it's a sin when we are drawn away and enticed by lust and give in to sin's desires which work death in us.

Both men and women are victims of sexual sin and exploitation. Both can be hustlers and try to seduce the opposite sex, not because they love them, but are seeking to satisfy their selfish lusts through them. Whoever is doing the hustling is degrading their target. This woman on the billboard was trying to hustle me, or any man who would give in to her. She was being exploited herself to play the harlot to the world for money. I hold to the conviction that it's spiritual warfare to seduce men and women into immorality.

Guys who are trying to live a pure life feel degraded by visual assaults and seductiveness the same way a woman feels degraded when she is objectified by lustful staring, or when her man has wandering eyes or a porn addiction. Remember, she wants to be pursued for her heart, not just her body. A wife with a porn-addicted husband can feel devalued in her self-image thinking she's not enough for her man.

This is the devil lying to her because no one is ever enough for sexual addiction. It has nothing to do with her beauty or value. Her man's brokenness is the problem at that point, not hers. No one feminine beauty is enough for a sex addict. For the female struggler, no one man can fulfill her fantasies. Not that romance novels or daydreaming are sin — it's what's going on in the imagination that matters. In either case, is energy being stolen from the marriage? Is the intimacy between the two of you being violated?

Choosing a Response

Back to the billboard; I shouted at the image of the woman, the devil, and God, restating my consecration and commitment to God and purity. I declared the word of God, *My body is for the Lord and not for sexual immorality. Devil, you will never own me again, and I will not conform to your gutter standard* (1 Cor. 6:13).

The devil is assaulting us for exploitation when he tempts us to do something we were not created for. We defeat him on the grounds of his temptation when we declare *what* we are for — purity, not immorality, and who we are for — the Lord — not the devil. Jesus defeated the devil this way with the word of God when he declared it to the tempter who was after his worship. (Mt 4:4-10) We succeed when we use Jesus' model.

Romans 12:2 speaks of presenting our bodies as a living sacrifice holy and acceptable to him and not being conformed to the world, but being transformed by the renewing of our minds. If I were conforming to the world's immoral standard, I would have pulled my van into the parking lot and gone inside to enjoy the view, after all — everyone else is.

Once again, the proud devil had overplayed his hand, his seduction only solidifying my resolve to submit to God and resist him. (James 4:7).

"My son, give me your heart [i.e., consecrate your heart], and let your eyes observe my ways. For a harlot is a deep pit, and a seductress is a narrow well. She also lies in wait as for a victim [addict], and increases the unfaithful among men" (Prov. 23:26–28).

The woman on the billboard was increasing "the unfaithful among men." She was selling herself out, exploited to increase the devil's inmate count in his sexual prison. I know she wasn't the devil because,

> [W]e do not wrestle against flesh and blood, but against principalities, against powers, against the rulers of the darkness of this age, against spiritual hosts of wickedness in the heavenly places. (Eph. 6:12)

The passage in Ephesians continues with a call to put on the whole spiritual armor of God so we can defeat the devil and stand in the evil day.

Sexual compromise is Satan's favorite tool in the bag because he knows if he can control our sexual desires, he can twist us to his will. He doesn't fight fair; he knows our history and seeks the vulnerability found in our weakest places to take us down.

Myth: Just give me sex and I'll be fine.

Another marriage myth is that, *once married, they'll get enough sex at home and any ongoing struggle with temptation and lust will end.* They think fidelity will be no problem as their battles will evaporate because, *Well, now I'm married.* People thinking this get discouraged at how hard it is to keep their hearts clean.

Wait, I thought marriage would end this.

Even if you married sexual Superman or Wonder Woman, and most of us didn't, temptation doesn't go away. It just doesn't work that way. We all wish it did. Even the well-fed are vulnerable.

Becoming sexually active in marriage can actually increase the desire for more, instead of curbing our appetites. Once married, we're allowed to have sex now so we may want it more often than our spouse, a universal source of conflict. If fidelity was easy, we wouldn't have this proverb warning us: "Drink water from your own cistern, and running water from your own well" (Prov. 5:15).

Neil Anderson states in his book *The Christ-Centered Marriage*, "Sexual bondage destroys many marriages, and the origin of the problem can usually be traced to pornography, promiscuity, incest and rape before marriage. Getting married will not resolve it. In many cases, the problem becomes accentuated."[1]

Take the Way of Escape

"No temptation has overtaken you except as is common to man; but God is faithful, who will not allow you to be tempted beyond what you are able, but will with the temptation make the way of escape, that you may be able to bear it" (1 Cor. 10:13).

One hot day I was home alone and went to the mailbox for the mail, and the devil had a letter just for me in the form of a racy summer clothing catalog.

I was alone and vulnerable, and the goddesses sent were worthy of admiration, yes, even worship. At one glance, maybe two, I knew radical measures were needed (Matt. 5:29–30).

I wasn't about to take it inside and burn incense at the altar of sexual idolatry. Instead, I carried it to the garage, found a metal bucket, and lit it on fire. I worshipped the Father as I watched it burn, and declared my consecration to him while the incense of my offering went up.

My way of escape this time was burning up the devil's bait sent to defeat me. I desecrated his altar with fire, refusing to unlock demonic doors and let strongholds into my mind (2 Chron. 34:5).

There was no thunder or burst of wind, but I imagined applause in heaven and the pleasure and validation of the Father. I rejoiced in the grace and resolve he had given me. The door was closed, and the devil left until a more opportune time, which I am not going to give him.

Loyalty to God is expressed by putting him in the high place in our hearts. With his grace and empowerment, we say no to the devil and bring our fleshly desires to the cross — reckoning them dead to sin, then worship him as we are raised in newness of life (Rom. 6:4).

Surrender to God—Then Fight

God does expect us to surrender our sexual selves to him to be delivered from sexual bondage. After the surrender, he then expects us to take up the battle against any habits we've developed through using our sex out of his will — using porn

156

or participating in the immorality of any kind. He wants *us* to conquer shame and fight for the ground we've yielded to find our freedom from sin.

He calls us to shed the victim role and take responsibility for our self-made mess. We assume the victim role when we blame our sin on whatever happened to us that causes us to live morally runaway lives. We shed this role through repentance and closing doors. He doesn't make the devil go away; he empowers us to defeat him. We must resist the devil and make him flee (James 4:7–10). God doesn't shrink the devil so we can win; he increases Christ in us for victory — He makes us bigger than the devil (1 Jn. 5:4,18).

Win Victory Over Porn

I couldn't gain victory over pornography until I saw it as idolatry, and I was worshipping the demons behind porn. I would gain some ground and win some battles but couldn't quite get free — my eye-gate wasn't pure. I couldn't repent deeply enough for freedom until I saw the moral and spiritual consequences of idolatry. By engaging in it, I was giving away my spiritual authority over my body and my passions. It was more serious than I realized.

I learned about spiritual warfare and doors needing to be closed before I could find freedom from my pornography addiction. It wasn't going to be quick or easy, but I began seeing breakthroughs and freedom as I closed doors. I closed them by repenting and renouncing the demonic spirits behind sexual idolatry. I committed my sexuality to

Jesus at deeper levels that brought his power to bear over my life. I made new resolves to once and for all be done with all sexual impurity.

I was imprisoned worse than I realized, and stronger measures were needed for these chains to break. I needed a spiritual confrontation to free areas of sexual brokenness. I needed to break and bind strongholds and imaginations, through the power of the blood of Jesus and the cross. I stopped permitting myself and surrendered my will to God anew. I developed a zero-tolerance policy for porn of any kind. No visuals whatsoever. I could behold the beauty of God's creation and appreciate it — but not to objectify. God's powerful grace and presence enable this.

Through Desert Stream Ministries and the Living Waters program, my eyes were opened to see the demonic influences surrounding sexual addiction and idolatry. This was more than a bad habit. I couldn't get off the sticky spider's web. It was spiritual bondage. There were "strongmen" to be bound, and their houses spoiled. The thief stole from me, and I had some property — my heart — to take back (John 10:10). My will had been taken captive by the devil for his use and it was time to get it realigned and empowered for God (2 Tim. 2:26).

I realized that whenever I viewed porn or fantasized sex in my mind, I was worshipping demons by bowing my knees at the altars of Baal and Ashtoreth. It could no longer be just "good clean fun," not that it ever was. It was idol worship, directly connected to demonic oppression. No wonder I couldn't break free!

I found a book on sexual purity called *At the Altar of Sexual Idolatry* that helped me see that sin is not static but progresses toward death (James 1:13–15).[2] I saw that our sexuality is also not static but depends on how we use it. There are laws around our sexuality. When it's misused in sexual immorality there is a downward progression. Our sexuality is powerful, and we work righteousness or unrighteousness in the way we use it.

I saw that my idolatry (I had to call it that), wasn't just a little sinful compartment in my otherwise spiritual life, as many sex addicts, even porn-viewing Christians, believe. It was harlotry, with the power and ability to rot me to the core, take me over, and separate me from God (Prov. 6:26).

I had to see sin as "exceedingly sinful" to repent deeply enough to get free (Rom. 7:13). I needed to see my distraction as an obsession of the mind and heart, not the playful game the devil makes it out to be. He whispers — *A little on the side never hurt anyone, who's gonna know?*

Reading this book on sexual idolatry strengthened my resolve to tear down the high place of sexual sin in my life — the strongholds in my mind and emotions — and keep renouncing the idolatry involved in pornography or looking at any woman lustfully.

As I held nothing back and gave my sexuality to Jesus and sought him for wisdom and wholeness, I felt an empowering resolve I didn't have before. I found my will empowered to *choose* his altar and *reject* the devil's. When we give our will to Jesus, He takes it away from the devil. The devil couldn't stop me as long as I submitted myself to Jesus and resisted him (James 4:7).

I began having power encounters with the Holy Spirit — and still do — that secure the core of my spirit and body because I am joined to him as one spirit (1 Cor. 6:17). This *joining* imparts spiritual empowerment as I yield to his power and give him everything. Sin was losing its grip over me, and my joy returned when I locked shame behind closed doors and threw away the keys.

We can't taper off sinning, we must be done with it. I realized we can't just reduce our time at false altars—they have to be removed and destroyed, or they will compel us to return to worship them. Because of the bondage connected to them, we can't just throw a sheet over them until later or we will be seduced back to them.

Like King Josiah in the Bible, these altars had to be destroyed to loosen their demonic hold (2 Chron. 34:3-7). They didn't just go away; they needed to be removed forcefully, and all the doors closed (Matt. 11:12). Only then could the people return to God with their whole hearts.

It helped me break free when God showed me what was happening in my heart. I had been giving my love for God away to other gods. My desire had been seduced and captured. It was spiritual harlotry. Adultery.

I couldn't say *I love God* and love Baal at the same time. When you are *loving* Baal, you can't be loving God. You cannot serve two masters (Matt. 6:24). We like to think we can serve sexual sin and say we're loving God, but we're not. We've gone into denial and left God's altar for the other.

It's hard to write about the subject of sexual idolatry. It's an upstream swim against the moral current of the day. The devil doesn't like people finding out how to get free. My wife Linda, just left the house to run some errands, and I called after her, "See you later. I'll be here writing about the sexual perversion of the world." We both laughed out loud at the irony and truth of it all.

Bind the Strongman

When we choose repentance, we change our altar of worship. Where we used to go to meet our needs through sexual sin, we make unavailable to ourselves by whatever means necessary. We make an end of it, or we haven't truly repented. The part of our heart we gave to idols, we offer anew to God on his altar that we have repaired. There will be no more playing around. We are plucking out our eyes and cutting off hands that are causing us to sin (Mt.5:29,30).

We tell God we are sorry we have played the harlot and given our hearts away. We "acknowledge our transgressions and our sin is ever before us" (Ps. 51:3, author's paraphrase).

Jesus said, "No one can enter a strong man's house and plunder his goods, unless he first binds the strong man. And then he will plunder his house" (Mark 3:27).

According to Jesus, there are strongmen that we are called to bind, then to enter their houses and plunder their goods. This isn't spooky, but practical when it comes to dealing with spiritual oppression and demonic influence. The strongman is the devil or demonic spirits that create and control strongholds in people. A stronghold is a prison that takes over our will and binds us through our thinking and actions. We are told to bind the strongman, and then we "plunder his house," when we drive out the demons and oppression in our lives. Jesus and his disciples did this regularly as a part of their ministry, and he called and empowered us to do the same in the ministry of discipleship (Mark 16:15-18).

Although there are many unclean and lustful spirits, two stand out to me as formidable strongmen. They are the spirit of Idolatry and the spirit of Harlotry.

Sexual idolatry is the strongman binding many among us. This is the actual worship involved in illicit sexual practices. When we give our sex away outside of the boundaries, we open ourselves to the power of the demons controlling the altar. These demons and gods were named after the high places that Israelites frequented (i.e., Baal and Ashteroth). There were many others we can't mention here.

The idolatry element compelled the worshipper to return to the altar to "burn incense" there to the demon behind the altar. The "worship" involved immoral sexual practices.

There were often sexual symbols present: the poles were phallic symbols, and there were obscene images related to Ashteroth and Baal. This is similar to the sexual images so prevalent and available today to encourage and enable worship of these same spirits.

A spirit of harlotry is another strong man fueling porn addiction and promiscuity (sexual looseness, sex without boundaries). Harlotry is the spirit that drives people to have multiple sexual partners, whether physically or mentally in their imaginations.

Hosea was a prophet who was told by God to marry a prostitute, to illustrate how his people were committing adultery against him by their idol worship. He says, "Harlotry, wine, and new wine enslave the heart. . . For the spirit of harlotry has caused them to stray, and they have played the harlot against their God" (Hos. 4:11–12).

The spirit of idolatry is the committing of sexual sin; the spirit of harlotry causes unfaithful straying. These two spirits work together and must be bound, to spoil their house and plunder their goods.

The following two prayers are designed to bind these two strongmen and spoil their houses. The prayers help you consecrate yourself, affirm your choice to worship God and find freedom from shame and strongholds in your life by renouncing the altar of Baal. These prayers make it clear to whom we belong, and that our bodies, hearts, and minds are for God and purity.

Consecration Statement

Dear Jesus,

I choose You now as my Lord and Savior. I see that You have bought me with the price of Your blood. Because of this, I will glorify You with my body and with my spirit, which both belong to You (1 Cor. 6:20). I enter now into a covenant with You concerning my sexuality.

I close the door, and I will not make myself available to sexual sin in mind or body, in any of its forms. I will not engage in sexual fantasy or masturbation. I will not dishonor my body with another sexually (Rom. 1:24). I present my body to You as a living sacrifice now on Your holy altar. Please let Your fire fall now and burn away any chains of sexual bondage.

Protect me in the secret place where You are my refuge and my fortress (Ps. 91). Be present to my heart and my weakness, and heal and protect me there. I trust You. Hide Your Word in my heart that I might not sin against You. Create in me a clean heart, O God, and renew a right spirit within me (Rom. 12:1; Ps. 119:9–11; Ps. 51).

In Jesus' name, amen.

Renouncing the Altar of Baal

Jesus gives us the authority to do this in Mark 16:17, so we can proceed without fear. Take time with this, and let the Holy Spirit work in your heart. These are prayers of self-deliverance and renunciation of demonic oppression related to sexual idolatry. This can be prayed out loud either alone, with a friend, or in a group.

Dear heavenly Father,

I come to You in Jesus' name. Thank You for Your love and mercy. Thank You for Jesus and the power of the cross that breaks sin's power. Thank You for the blood that cleanses me, forgives me, and declares me righteous before Your throne. Thank You, Jesus, for pursuing and reclaiming my heart. Thank You, Holy Spirit, for being here now in power. God has not given me a spirit of fear, but love, power, and a sound mind.

"No one can enter a strong man's house and plunder his goods, unless he first binds the strong man. And then he will plunder his house" (Mark 3:27).

In this part—using Jesus' model, we speak directly to spirits that have had control over us and we verbally challenge and break their power (Luke 9:1; 10:17–19). These are prayers of authority and declaration to be prayed in faith—knowing God has given you authority and is backing you up with the spiritual power of his kingdom (Matt. 16:19).

I now bind the strongman of sexual idolatry in the name of Jesus, and I spoil your house, the house of sexual idolatry. Your grip–the demonic grip of sexual idolatry—over me has ended, and I break its power over my life, mind, and body in Jesus' name. I renounce all spirits of sexual uncleanness, perversion, adultery, and harlotry and break their power over me.
I bind the strongman of harlotry, and I spoil your house of harlotry through the cross and blood of Jesus Christ who defeated you. I command you to leave me now in Jesus' name. You are cut off from me and lose your power over me from this point on.

I renounce the spirit of seduction, assigned to tempt me and weaken me with sexual sin. Leave me now— with your influence—in Jesus' name. I renounce pornography and fantasy in all its forms. I am done with you. My eye is single, and my body is full of light.

I break all soul ties and false one-flesh sexual covenants I have ever made in my life. I break any shame or defilement coming from those past unions, and I place the cross between them and me. I claim the redeeming power of the cross of Jesus. Thank You, Jesus; you make all things new — the past cannot torment me.

I put the cross of Jesus Christ between me and my past sexual history, and also between me and the sins of my forefathers. I ask forgiveness, Father, for the sins of my ancestors and ask You to disempower any generational curses that have flowed to me because of them.

I renounce the altars of sexual idolatry, including Baal and Ashtoreth, and cut off the influence of all spirits of sexual perversion connected to them. I declare they have no power over me to influence my mind, emotions, or sexual desires. I break and renounce all covenants and agreements with sexual idolatry I have ever made. I put them under the blood and declare they no longer have any power over me.

I will not worship at the altar of sexual idolatry. I renounce lust in all its forms and will keep my eye and ear gates pure so that my whole body may be full of light (Matt. 6:22–23).

Jesus, I give myself to You now, spirit, soul, and body. I am Yours, resting in the shadow of Your cross. My life is hidden with You.

I thank You now, Jesus, for removing any legal ground the devil or demons have had to oppress my life in this area. Thank You for sanctifying my sexuality through the power of Your blood and Your cross. I renounce all guilt, shame, and condemnation. They must leave me now in the name of Jesus. I receive Your grace and empowerment.

I receive Your complete cleansing and forgiveness. I let Your blood speak for me. I also forgive myself for all past sexual sins and the choices I have made. Thank You for the joy of a forgiven and clean heart. Thank You for setting me free! Thank You for the hope for a free life! In Jesus' name — Amen!

CHAPTER ELEVEN

Banish the Differences Myth

*When we give people the freedom to disagree with us,
we are giving them the freedom to be human.*

—Gary Chapman

Differences have the potential to create intimacy. If we see our differences as a wall, we will try to remove them. If we see them as the doorway, we will search for the key.

A myth that disconnects marriages is that our differences are bad and we need to remove them. The myth supports the lie that conflict and power struggles are destructive and need to be avoided at all costs. We will reject differences as obstacles and try to change our partners. This breaks the connection when your partner feels the pain of your pressure to change them, and withdraws.

We find our connection through validating differences and exploring them. We are challenged to change our point of view about our different ways of handling power and conflict.

Honor Your Differences

The good news is that Jesus will heal the pain in marriage when we start talking about our differences and strategizing together how to navigate them. We can't love our spouse unless we learn to honor these differences.

More good news is that exploring and understanding our differences leads to intimacy and passion. The more we can identify and understand our differences and the needs they represent — the more satisfaction is found through honoring and caring for them.

Our differences are the energy for committed love. Two powerful people learning to honor and respect differences is a force that will electrify feelings of love. The connection our hearts are craving is found in the ongoing journey of validating and embracing our differences — and opening the doors to intimacy they represent.

Polarization and Acceptance

Polarization begins when the honeymoon period ends and the power struggle begins. Dazzled at first with new love, we are filled with unrealistic expectations of what our partner is going to provide for us—of who they are going to be for us.

Polarization pulls us into reality to finally accept the way things are going to be based on reality, and not the romance myths we've been believing—the fairy tale thinking we've had.

Because of how painful this is when our dreams of what could have been die, we can't imagine how God could be involved at all. Good emotions subside as others take over, and two who once felt unified end up feeling alienated and alone. Suddenly seeing how different we are, we're *repelled* by these differences. What first attracted us now pushes us away from each other.

Why do we need this polarization?

We need polarization because God won't allow us to have a fake marriage based on illusions.

We need the gift of polarization because we've fallen in love with a romanticized image of our spouse and not the real person. We are forced through polarizing to see ourselves and our spouses as they really are—not through the love fog. We've seen how the love drug is powerful and convinces us that this person is the answer to all we need. This image of them as our savior can easily become an idol, as we worship our idealized image of our lover. We end up loving an image of them—the one we've created to serve us.

A type of this illusion is revealed in a scene from the movie Notting Hill. Julia Roberts is in Hugh Grant's book store inviting him deeper into a relationship with her. He feels that he has been dismissed by her, and is telling her that they are from two different worlds. She is a famous movie star, and he is a commoner.

He uses this argument as grounds to tell her *no — he can't risk it*. She knows he can only see his *image* of her and not the real person, and says, "The fame thing isn't real you know — I'm also a girl standing in front of a boy — asking him to love her."[1]

He saw only the *image* of who she was, the famous actress Anna Scott, and not the vulnerable girl who wanted to have a normal love relationship with him outside the ring of fame.

Isn't this a reflection of us in marriage, standing before one another, vulnerably offering our hearts, but so ready to flee the risk of pain involved in loving with abandon?

Perhaps this fear of risk explains why we go to the towers. When we love an image of who we want them to be, we aren't loving the real person. Our eyes must be opened so we can be freed from our self-centered motives for love. We can then grow to love the person and not the image.

With the fading of eros love, our delusions of reality can be exposed. Another reason we need to polarize is that initially, we see our partner as an extension of ourselves. Polarization pushes us out of our enmeshment emotionally so we can see ourselves apart from them.

We must grow to love them as separate from ourselves, loving and affirming who *they are*, before we can unite with them in oneness. As we are humbled in this process, we will discover our motivations have been rather self-centered.

Polarization is a gift with the potential for growth and healing. God is asking us to give up what feels good now for a better thing we can't see yet. He is asking us to trust that he is good — and our marriage isn't ruined or over now, because we have to die to some things and it's time for the work to begin. This takes commitment indeed. We must forsake gratification now for something in the future that hasn't materialized yet. We obey "by faith." "By faith, Abraham obeyed when he was called to go out—and he went out—not knowing where he was going" (Heb. 11:8).

Your Spouse— a Problem or Passageway?

The things we resist about each other can be the doorways to joy and intimacy. Instead of trying to remove the door, we're invited to walk through it, embrace new insights about each other in the process, and travel a more satisfying path together.

You and your beloved aren't obstacles to what each of you wants, rather, you are the passageway into what each other wants and needs. You are God's gifts to each other, and love is what lights this passageway.

I can view Linda as an obstacle to what I want or as a beautiful soul with her own needs and desires. I can view her as a project to be shaped to serve me, or as a tender heart standing in front of me needing love and understanding.

I can ask myself in frustration,

Why is she acting this way? What's wrong with her? Why is she resisting me?

Or I can choose to step back, look within, and gain God's perspective on what's going on. When I have his point of view, I will ask better questions, ones not focused on me:

> *What does she need that I'm not giving her? Where is she afraid and needs my reassurance? Where is she hurting or struggling and needing my support?*

I can choose to see her as the woman God gave me to love, honor, and understand. I can choose to stop pushing my agenda, die at times to what I want and need, and listen and love. The attitude I choose shapes how I treat her, feel about her, and relate to her which will define my marriage.

If I believe the myth that differences are bad and need to be removed, I will try to change my partner into what I want them to be. This sets up a relational battlefield as my partner withdraws from my control and change efforts.

However, if we can form healthy relating patterns early and engage truthfully, our joy and intimacy can only grow. Our spouses want to connect with us when we invite them to explore with us in a safe and gentle environment.

Our goal is to learn to handle our differences in a godly, redemptive way. Yes, it hurts when we're disappointed. Yes, there are tears when we feel abandoned, frustrated, or aren't getting what we need. But only by surrendering to God's way of doing things in our marriage are we going to find fulfillment.

We can reach the place where we tell ourselves, *I am not going to try to change them or control them. I'm going to learn with Your help, God, to love them just the way they are. I will let You change me. Whatever You want, I surrender, I trust you with them.*

When we can say that and mean it, we are working with God instead of trying to work around him. When our hands are open, his hands can move to transform both of us.

Acknowledge Your Fear

Why do we resist the differences the way we do, then obsess with changing them?

Because of our fear. We feel the threat of losing something important to us. This compels us to control and protect what we're afraid of losing. We won't stop controlling until we can identify the fear driving our control. Look for the fear. When you find it, you'll discover what you're fighting about.

Drs. Les and Leslie Parrot, in their insightful book *Love Talk*, write, "Each and every one of us has a fear of losing something we value in the daily exchanges of our relationship. We may fear losing time, approval, loyalty, or quality."[2]

They go on to explain these four things we are most fearful of losing:

1. gaining control of time
2. winning approval from others
3. maintaining loyalty
4. achieving quality standards

We will tend to value one or two of these things above the others, even though we may value all of them to some extent. The fear of losing these values will cause us to resist the differences in our partner that threaten us.

Here are examples of how these four fuel the conflicts:

1. If I fear losing time, I become anxious when something is taking longer than it should and I will try to control the situation so I don't *lose* control of time. An example is given just ahead.
2. If I fear losing the approval of others, I become anxious in a relationship if I perceive they will disapprove of us because of the choices we are making. I will be tempted to control the dynamic to ensure the approval I fear losing.

3. If maintaining loyalty is a value, anxiety leading to control will surround any situation that would communicate disloyalty to those I value or love. We will explore this further in chapter 13.

4. If I fear losing the quality standard I value, anxiety increases when I'm pushed to decide or do something that is below my standard. An example of this is just ahead as well.

Understand and Honor Your Differences

Ben and Mary are newlyweds. They've been married six months, and the honeymoon glow isn't gone, but the shine has dimmed. It's not what it was.

Ben has noticed something that bothers him: Mary needs more connection and involvement than he's comfortable giving. His personality is laid-back, and he feels pressured by Mary's drive. She never seems to stop and is often trying to get him to *do* something.

He feels anxious when she's around, can't relax, and feels he doesn't have permission to rest. She seems to get bored, starts new projects, and then wants his involvement. He feels like he can't get a break.

This wears him out, and he needs space to recharge, so he withdraws from her. Their personalities are different, and so are their needs and how they try to meet them.

Mary notices Ben seems to be pulling away from her and feels the emotional distance this is creating. This pushes her insecurity button and compels her to cling to him more. She doesn't like how it feels. His withdrawal magnifies her fear, so she tries to connect with Ben by finding projects for him to do.

> Their mutual fear dance intensifies.
> She thinks, *Doesn't he love me anymore?*
> He thinks, *I just need some room to breathe.*

> The insecurity of their towers is calling.

Is this his problem or hers? If you said both, you're right. Do you remember the line from the movie *Apollo 13*, "Houston, we have a problem"? That line applies very much to marriage. *We* have a problem. It's not you or me, it's *us*. The process of becoming one with another person is taking the journey *together* to solve problems *we* have, whatever they are.

In other words, the problem belongs to both Ben and Mary. Her issue is connection. She needs more, he needs less. His issue is depletion. He needs space to retreat to what Mark Gungor calls the Nothing Box — Neil Anderson calls them caves. This is where guys typically go to recharge, reset, and process.

She thinks he's spaced out and not present. He's not even thinking about it — he's simply recharging by disconnecting for a while. Guys just aren't full-on all the time like their women can seem to be. Both sexes are created differently in this way.

It helps to remember that Adam was in the garden with God before Eve. The masculine side of man possesses a certain "call of the wild," which the woman may not relate to or understand. Not a detached Marlboro Man, but connected with freedom. Not freedom to a life apart from her, but freedom to disconnect occasionally for a time to recharge. This makes him available for a more quality connection she may seek.

Both men and women need healthy relationships of the same sex outside the marriage as well. He may not be the best recreational companion at the opera, tea party, or ballet. She may not be the best outward-bound companion. I knew the first time I took Linda skiing with me that this just wasn't going to happen. She tried. We have to explore different things and find out what works for us.

He needs her companionship, love, and validation, but she can smother him by keeping him in a nonstop connection. Men need to recharge and have different ways of doing this — usually involving getting away from her for a while. The security needs to be developed in the marriage to make this possible.

We mustn't attack these differences but understand and honor them to maintain our connection and not push each other away by disapproval and invalidation. Attacking our differences is what puts us in our towers.

So how can Ben meet his need to recharge while reassuring Mary he's not abandoning her? At the same time, how can Mary meet her need for connection while giving Ben the space he needs? Both of these questions are the doorway to discovery about each other and what we both need. The tension and often conflict come because we *are* different.

The differences myth we are banishing is that differences are wrong and we need to change them. We navigate differences successfully when we understand them and honor them, not try to remove them. For starters, Ben can honor Mary by meeting her need for reassurance so she can understand his withdrawal. He must first get in touch with his needs, unpack the anxiety behind them, and then talk with Mary about what he needs without attacking or blaming her.

This is a challenge for us at first because we aren't used to unpacking feelings and understanding our related dynamics. The couple needs to secure the castle by disarming their fears and making it safe for each other to disclose. Mary will need to create other ways of connecting with Ben that don't involve putting him to work. He can help her but needs other ways of connecting.

She can choose to join him in some activities that recharge him so in return he can then help her, but from a recharged place. They will have to work out together the details of what this looks like for them. The things they could decide on depend on what recharges each of them. Typically what charges up one depletes another, so we need to give and take. There is a list of replenishers and depleters at the back of the book. When you talk about them together, you can agree on some you could try.

In our marriage, I enjoy live music — especially jazz and blues. Going to an occasional concert is great for me, and Linda enjoys them. You have to park and fight crowds and so on, but it can also be fun. Then there's the opera or Trans-Siberian Orchestra! Or the seasonal *Scrooge*.

Golf is another recharger for me. Linda doesn't golf, but she enjoys riding along and loves getting outside. We enjoy movies together, trading off between Hallmark and sci-fi. We love going to dinner, which can be paired with another event or outing — possibly with another couple. We share ministry in our church and small groups. We help couples with marriage mentoring. We no longer have a tug of war but more of a gentle waltz, or slow dance.

Back to Ben and Mary . . . The more Mary understands what Ben needs, the more she can see that his withdrawal isn't fueled by a lack of love for her, but by his pain of feeling depleted.

The more Ben understands what Mary needs, the more he can reassure her in ways that don't leave him feeling depleted. It's a matter of understanding the needs that aren't being met. Conflicts usually arise from unmet needs that exist because they are unknown, misunderstood, or neglected. If we explore these conflicts instead of avoiding them we can discover how to meet these needs and feel loved.

The good news is that even though our needs are different, they can be met when understanding and love are present.

Meet the Needs Beneath the Differences

Let me tell you about another couple.

Rachel is down to business with a structured personality. Ed is happy-go-lucky and unstructured. Rachel wants to plan things and get things done; Ed would rather leave their schedule open and let things unfold. Rachel is logical and practical; Ed is emotional and a processor.

Despite their differences, Rachel and Ed are very much in love, and the first few months of their marriage have been incredible. Rachel adores the ground Ed walks on and feels lucky to have an engaging man who cares for her and protects her the way he does — not to mention the fact that he's a great lover!

Ed, however, feels planned to death and can't breathe. Plus, he wants to talk to Rachel about feelings, which Rachel finds bothersome. Ed, who is contemplative and needs to process his emotions, is beginning to feel a distance between them.

He thinks to himself, *I don't feel loved by her. She doesn't care about what's going on in my heart. It feels like she's using me for what she wants, and I'm not getting what I need in return.*

Ed stops cooperating and starts pumping the brakes. He tells Rachel he isn't going to plow on to what's next until she honors what's going on in his heart by listening to him and processing some of his struggles with him.

Ed's comments leave Rachel feeling perplexed and uncomfortable. Reluctantly, she hears him out, trying to understand what he's talking about, and thinks to herself, *Can't we just get on with things? Why do we have to get bogged down with talking about feelings? Doesn't he see how much work needs to get done?*

Because she adores her husband, she promises to "try harder," but she doesn't have a clue what he's after or how to give it to him.

Their towers of unmet needs are calling.

How can Rachel meet her own need to function on a logical, practical plane while still hearing Ed, validating his feelings, and giving him the connection he needs? And how can Ed meet his need for processing and connection without driving Rachel away?

Accepting our differences and learning to love and respect each other's unique needs — even when they are very different from our own — is the answer.

Rachel needs to listen to Ed, give him some quality time, and let him process a little. Ed needs to understand that Rachel's "get 'er done" attitude meets her needs and is not a reflection of how she feels about him.

Our natural first impulse is to change our spouses to remove the tension we feel. This is "baby love," seeking to manipulate change to gain sameness between us. All marriages go through this. We think, *If I can change them, I won't have to navigate the discomfort they are causing me.*

Mature love, on the other hand, will explore to understand and meet the needs behind the tension. It's a love that says, *I will set aside my discomfort to understand what you need.* This process transforms us and we bond. No one is left alone in a tower when this happens. By exploring and honoring our differences, we remove the distance between us.

Allow Your Differences to Open the Door to Greater Love and Intimacy

When it comes to shopping, you may be familiar with this analogy of the classic differences between men and women. A man goes shopping like he goes deer hunting. He gets the animal in his sight, shoots it, bags it, and takes it home. It's a done deal. He only needs one, and it doesn't take looking at a lot to decide. Bagging the target and getting home is the goal.

Women, however, shop differently. For many women, the *experience* of shopping is the goal, and when they shop, they want to consider the options and take the time to choose. It's like taking a tour through the botanical gardens where you must see all the flowers so you don't miss anything. Nothing is fast about the process. Getting in and out as soon as possible isn't even on the table. Plus, shopping doesn't mean she will even bag anything (this is how window shopping was invented). Or shopping may mean she will come home with more than she had planned to buy.

Shopping with Linda became easier for me when I saw that achieving quality standards (i.e., taking her time to make the right finds) was her value while protecting my time was mine. I gained peace when I changed my perspective and tried to understand hers. I began to see shopping as something roman-tic I could do with her—like a date—instead of something I needed to get out of the way to protect my time.

I realized I needed to *give my time* to her so she could achieve the *quality standards* she needed to make a purchase. I needed to understand her need to try on as many dresses as necessary, rather than pushing her toward a choice. I could choose love by honoring her need for a quality choice.

The more I thought about my fear of losing valuable time, the more I began to think of it as irrational and selfish. Who owned my time anyway? Who was giving it to me to share with her? God was giving me this time to love and honor her.

And if giving her my time makes her feel loved and sup-ported, isn't that more important than other things I could spend my time on? I can always choose not to go and let her shop alone or with a girlfriend. But when I do go with her, it's intending to meet her needs, not my own.

My mindset when we shop together must be, *This is about her, not about me.* And then I look for a chair and occupy myself. When I do this, I discover that our different approaches to shopping have opened the door for me to grow in my love for her and to communicate that love.

Decision-making is the stuff of life, right? Which career path do I take? How should we prioritize our goals and our budget? Should we buy a bigger house? Which vehicle should we purchase and drive? What about insurance?

When we tackle our differences in how we make decisions, we can find agreement and minimize conflict. Our differences won't disappear. They are part of who we are and were put there by design and for a reason, to protect us and balance us.

CHAPTER TWELVE
Wield Words Well

Above all, people need to let go of counterproductive behaviors and replace them with more effective ones.

— Harville Hendrix

There is a verse in Proverbs that tells us how to create an established and treasure-filled life, home, and marriage:

By wisdom a house is built, and through understanding it is established; through knowledge its rooms are filled with rare and beautiful treasures. (Prov. 24:3 NIV). Wisdom is the master builder that establishes and enriches our marriages and homes. It's the project manager who oversees and coordinates the project. It does this by teaching us how to use life-giving words and attitudes that increase our understanding of each other. Our good words and attitudes establish a healthy home and create the quality of our connection.

Do you know what honeymoon words are? They are words of love, acceptance, and validation.

When we're newlyweds, we love everything we see about our spouses, and we tell them so. They are "so cute," and make us laugh. We are the center of each other's attention. Our words are kind and uplifting. We ask questions that help us understand each other and fall even more deeply in love.

The discovery process is so fun!

It's fun until we run into the walls of differing preferences and operating systems.

When this happens, honeymoon words often get replaced by more challenging words and conversations:

"Why are you doing it *that way?*"

"What do you mean? That's the way you're *supposed* to do it."

"That's not how *I* learned it."

"So you think *your* way is better?"

"I'm not saying that."

"Then what *are* you saying?"

"I guess I'm just not used to it being different and need to adjust."

"Is this going to happen every time I do something different than you?"

"Only if *my* way is better."

The truth is that as our marriage progresses, we need to be more intentional about our talk styles. We enter our marriages unequipped for the damage our broken words and styles create. Until we learn to confront and edit the words we say, we will sabotage our communication process. Your marriage experience is the fruit of all the words you speak to each other, whether those words are affirming or critical, accepting or demanding.

To change your words—and change your marriage—four questions need to be asked and answered.

1. The Work of My Words: What Are They Doing?

Every time you want to accomplish a *task* in a relationship, you will use words to get that job done, whatever it is. I like to say that words are hard workers, and I view them as employees to carry out the job I have for them. They can dig a ditch that carries life-giving water or poison, depending on how we use them.

Here's why words do so much:

- Words are not passive but active seeds, all possess inherent creative potential.
- Words determine our relational diet and are at work creating the fruit we will eat.
- Words work to create dynamics and emotions in our marriages, uniting or dividing.
- Words are containers with a delivery system. Like a syringe or virus delivers serum into the body, so words deliver life-giving or life-depleting serum into our spirits.
- Words have job descriptions and are always *doing* something; building up or tearing down, affirming or invalidating, inviting or pushing away.

Wisdom will help you ask before you speak, What is the work of the words I'm about to say? What will they accomplish, and how will they impact our connection and our environment? Do I want to use these words?

2. The Motive of My Words: Why Am I Choosing the Words I Choose?

Ask God to show you the *why* behind the words you use. What is your motive behind using *those* words? Is it to tear your spouse down, or build them up? Are you bullying, or inviting dialogue?

Relational Messages

Relational messages are the messages we send by our communication style—the words we use and the way we're using them. We can send disapproval or acceptance messages to our partner by our choice of words and tone of delivery.

For instance, imagine I'm sitting in my chair in the living room writing while my wife Linda is sitting on the couch. She starts playing a noisy computer game or watching a documentary featuring trumpeting elephants and it's irritating me. I think to myself—*really? I can't concentrate on my writing*. I'm irritated because she is disrupting my focus. I want my words to do the job of gaining me some peace, but the motive of my heart will choose the words I select.

If my motive is to get silence at any cost, I could carelessly say something like, "Do you have to make so much noise?" It's easy to see why that wouldn't go over well. That sends the message, You're noisy and irritate me. I wish you would go away. You bother me and are in the way. I'm only happy when you're seen and not heard.

These reckless words may get me the silence I seek, but they will wound Linda in the process. If I hurt her, she will withdraw from me and not want to be emotionally connected. The towers are waiting, and I will be sending us there. Then relational repair would be needed after I wrecked everything. Do you know that feeling? It's like she was the little girl splashing around in the wading pool, and I tipped the pool over and all the water ran out. She will cry because I wrecked everything.

Maybe I could say, "Can you please turn that down so I can write?"

That might seem a little better, but is it? Here's the relational accusing message: What I'm doing is more important than your silly game or obnoxious elephants. You're rude and inconsiderate, and blocking my goals for peace and quiet.

It does send the message that what I'm doing is more valuable than what she's doing, and she needs to adjust to me and stop. My unspoken relational message is that *I am the sun, you are the moon, and you need to orbit me quietly.* I would never say that in direct words, but my unspoken relational message can send it loud and clear.

Even if she stops what she's doing, I broke the connection between us with the proud, mean words I've used. I may get my silence, but will also reap the emotional distance and isolation I created because of the relational message I sent— *you bother me.* It contained a put-down and delivered negative emotions into her spirit.

If I have a habit of talking this way, I'm driving my wife away over and over. No wonder I feel lonely. She's not creating my reality, I am creating it by offending her. I'm building the tower, (our distance), and I need to own that for anything to change or get better. I own it when I see the words I'm using as the problem, instead of blaming her for *the way she is.*

Picking better words and styles keeps positive emotions alive between us and edits the bad feelings out. Yes, the words we choose and use create the emotional climate we live and breathe in, or suffocate and die in.

A better option is to say, "I've enjoyed hanging out with you, but I'm going into my office and digging into this chapter for a while. See you in a bit."

Relational Message sent: *I like your company, but I need some space, so I'm going away, but I'm looking forward to being with you later.*

With words like these, I can get what I need, solitude and quiet, without pushing her away in the process. I can take responsibility for getting what I need without using unloving words or reacting in irritation. After all, love is patient and kind. By "loving" instead of demanding, I don't let reckless, piercing words into our environment. I don't take away her freedom by trying to control her behavior.

Consider the words you tend to use. What insights do they give you into your motive for choosing them? To help with this, reflect on the following:

If I'm using my words to defend myself, they'll be defensive, justifying, and blustering. I can't listen and will rebut what's said to me. Words like these are motivated by insecurity when I feel threatened. Defensiveness is self-protection; my overexplaining is a giveaway to my insecurity and fear of being misunderstood or misjudged.

If I'm using my words to gain power over another, they'll be pushy, guilting, or controlling. These words come from the need to dominate to quell feelings of powerlessness. I fear letting another be in charge so I make sure they aren't. By giving away the power I end up retaining it because I'm giving it up for love, which is power, instead of using it for selfish purposes that degrade the one I love.

If I'm using my words to be right or win an argument, they'll be unyielding and aggressive. When I use these words I fear losing, forgetting that winning feels empty if it leaves another heart closed. Needing to win is about having the power. Think what could change if you let them win — besides, losing once in a while makes winning more enjoyable.

If I'm using my words to affirm and validate my spouse, my words will reflect what I appreciate about them or something positive I've observed. Words like these are motivated by love. My motive is for her to feel loved, valued, and respected by me — so I look for opportunities and ways I can express that. I could say things like. *You have value to me. I honor you. I see the sacrifice you make. I appreciate what you bring.*

Jesus says, "But the things that come out of a person's mouth come from the heart, and these defile them" (Matt. 15:18 NIV).

Yes, our words can defile us in our marriages. So before you speak, ask yourself, *What is the motive behind my words? Why am I choosing the words that I'm choosing? Where are these words going to leave us as a couple — connected — or in our towers?*

3. The Intentionality of My Words: Are My Words Reckless or Intentional?

The words of the reckless pierce like swords, but the tongue of the wise brings healing (Prov. 12:18 NIV).

Words from a wise tongue are like healing medicine that creates safety and encourages risk-taking. They help us succeed in exploring, resolving, and healing. Wise words lead to intimacy and connection. We can find these when wise tongues know how to speak healing words.

Reckless, careless words sabotage disclosure and make it unsafe to open up to a spouse. Reckless words pierce like swords, slashing and making us bleed. We may not realize the power and effect of our words.

Proverbs says that life and death are in the power of the tongue:

Words kill, words give life; they're either poison or fruit — you choose (Prov. 18:21 MSG).

All troubled marriages have in common reckless words. When we let God show us where our words are reckless, he will give us wise words to heal and build our houses instead of tearing them down.

There's probably more conflict at the front end of marriage because we haven't yet learned to talk right. I can remember a lot of explosions between Linda and me early on. We can all relate to having our buttons pushed and responding automatically out of angry, hurt emotions.

Marriage is an arena where we can get *all* our buttons pushed by our partners. We can feel exposed and defenseless before them as we are learning to fight fair. This is usually when reckless words come out of our mouths as we're caught off guard by one of our triggers.

We don't speak the best words when we are reacting rather than responding. We know the regret of having spoken words we wish we could take back. The good news is when we realize the power our words have, we can use them intentionally to build honoring and valuing relationships.

As we grow in God's grace, we find we don't have to react. With practice, we can learn to respond out of a graceful awareness that leads to self-control. As I get in touch with my emotions and what sets them off, I can slow down my responses and words. I can say to myself — *easy does it.* By putting myself in slow-motion mode, I can see what I'm doing and choose better.

Slowing down and responding intentionally allows me to consider my words carefully before I send them. It helps me to consider these questions to see my motives clearly before I speak,

- What are these words designed to do?
- Why am I thinking of sending them?
- What will their effect be on my spouse? Us? Is that worth it?
- What will I gain, or lose, from using these words?
- Are they loving? Or is it my flesh?
- Can I hold my breath and consider better ones?

4. The Power of My Words: Are My Words Giving Life or Death to My Spouse?

Are your words creating a path to connection and life or separation and death?

To be better equipped to use words that create a path to connection, try to understand, then accept these truths:

- ☐ I accept the truth that every time I speak to my spouse, the words I use send powerful messages about our relationship: "I accept you / I judge you." "I respect you / I disrespect you. "I affirm you / I invalidate you."
- ☐ I accept the truth that these unspoken messages evoke emotions in my spouse — positive or negative, causing my spouse to be attracted to me or repelled.
- ☐ I accept the truth that our words to each other evoke emotions that create the climate in which we live.
- ☐ I accept the truth that if we want intimacy and closeness, we have to send relational messages that invite and unite, not push away and divide.

Remember, words are containers that carry messages in them that nourish or deplete. They approve or disapprove, criticize or affirm, honor or degrade, bring life or death. They apply pressure to perform, or they extend grace. When we can grasp the truths above, it can change everything about how we feel living together.

Here's an example from my marriage. Since I tend toward perfectionism and performance, I have to choose words that don't put unreasonable demands and expectations on Linda. And by sowing grace to her, I will reap grace from her. I want grace-driven environments in our marriages, not performance-driven ones like the world offers.

The other day Linda said in a self-recriminating tone, *I forgot to deposit those checks in the bank.*

I could have voiced disappointment or agreed with her self-condemnation by remaining silent — or I could have fought for her heart.

Here's what I chose to say: That's okay, we'll get them in there tomorrow. It's not like it's going to break the bank. Don't be so hard on yourself — you've got a lot on your plate.

This relational message filled our environment with grace and took the pressure off Linda, who can be too hard on herself. When we are one, what one is feeling the other feels also. When we fight for our spouse we are fighting for ourselves. (Eph. 5:28-33)

We find life when we show mercy to each other and sow it into the marriage. Grace brings relief to a performance-driven environment.

CHAPTER THIRTEEN

Break the Chains of Dysfunctional Relationships

We were not meant to be enslaved by each other; we were meant to love each other freely.

—Dr. Henry Cloud

The year was 1978, and I had a newborn son. I was so excited about being a dad! At twenty-one, I barely had any idea what I was doing, but I worked hard to be a good provider and father. I had Dad's example of the love of a good father to me and my seven siblings. I knew I could be that for my son.

When I was offered an out-of-town job opportunity, my wife encouraged me to go, promising to join me in a couple of weeks. I moved, and about the time she was to join me with our son, I received divorce papers instead. She had never intended to follow.

I felt devastated and betrayed.

For the following nine years, I held on in faith that the marriage would be restored, to the point of choosing not to hire a lawyer and to defend myself in court. As a result, I lost visiting privileges with my son and was assaulted with court papers for years.

I not only lost my dream of happily ever after but also the dream of raising my son. This was a hefty price to pay. Grief devastated me. Was I destined to spend my life defined by bitterness and loss? Wounds we've received from toxic relationships, render us unable to live and love in the freedom God provides for us.

If you've been through a divorce, you have what I call an ex-file. If your parents or children have divorced, you have an ex-file. Anyone divorcing whose relational fallout affects you creates an ex-file for you. This file contains all the emotions involving the ex.

There may be no other file in life that contains more pain, unresolved issues, and unanswered questions than the ex-file. It's one we wish we didn't have, let alone have to dig into. But dig into it we must if we are to find the power to forgive and heal from the trauma involved. We can move out of denial, come to acceptance, and let Jesus redeem and heal.

God says he *hates divorce* (Mal. 2:16) — and rightly so, considering the treachery and fallout involved. Children are separated from fathers, mothers, grandparents, and family support systems. Hearts are broken and dreams die.

And unfortunately, these kinds of life-altering wounds aren't limited to divorce. Sometimes they come from past or current dysfunctional relationships with parents, siblings, friends, people in authority over us, and even adult children.

I met a woman last week who is planning a wedding to her longtime partner and the father of their twelve-year-old son. I asked why they had waited so long to marry.

She said she had been filled with too much anger over her toxic relationship with her abusive mother. She explained that her anger had left her unable to open up to anyone and that as a result, her relationship with her partner had been more about logistics than intimacy.

"What changed?" I probed.

"Last year Jeff, my fiancé, and I lost someone close to us from cancer. Somehow that grief opened the door to all my grief and anger over my mom. As I began to let go of some of that, Jeff and I began to open up emotionally to each other in ways we never had. I still have a lot of anger at my mom, but I don't want to let it keep me from living my own life anymore."

God wants to free us from chains to hurts from past or even current relationships. We can't go back and redeem our past. We must let Jesus be the *Lord of the past,* as Bob Bennett sings about in his song with the same name.

Let's take a look at three things we can do to begin to surrender these strongholds to Jesus and find the freedom and wholeness we long to experience.

1. Make a Decision to Forgive

Peter asked Jesus a question we've all asked: Lord, how often shall my brother sin against me, and I forgive him? Up to seven times? (Matt. 18:21).

I love Peter's depth of spiritual insight and desire for spiritual growth. His question to Jesus is not a surface one. To ask this question, *how often,* shows that Peter is thinking about unforgiveness. Perhaps he's dealing with a difficult person and is struggling with forgiving him.

He's saying, in essence, How far do we go with this forgiveness thing, Jesus? Up to seven times? That should do it, he probably figured.

But Jesus' answer sets an entirely different bar for forgiveness. Jesus said to him, "I do not say to you, up to seven times, but up to seventy times seven" (Matt. 18:22).

This same Jesus would go on to give his life on the cross and lay it down for all mankind. Our ability to forgive is found in gazing at the crucified one who set the standard. We forgive because he forgave us.

You may need to forgive as your heart breaks and you watch your dreams die. Chances are you won't simply need to forgive once. You may find yourself needing to forgive seventy times seven. And then some! Despite the pain that comes from chapters of brokenness in our lives, we know that our Redeemer is mighty, making all things new.

The cross provides the power to forgive others for anything. Jesus asks his followers to live out his example of forgiveness.

This will ensure a heart free to love, not chained and tormented by the bitterness of unforgiveness.

And Jesus' words to Peter do something else. They set the bar so high that we can't do it on our own. If we are to forgive—and keep forgiving—people who hurt us deeply, our *only* choice is to go to the cross and seek the help of Jesus.

Forgiveness involves the healing of damage done through the betrayal of another. I was so wounded by the fallout of my first marriage that the only way to escape a life of bitterness was to turn to Jesus daily and ask for his help and empowerment. I brought Him into my pain.

This is more than a choice to forgive. We can only forgive from the heart as we bring our wounded hearts to him for his love and healing. We can't wall off from the pain; we must let Jesus into it.

2. Practice Setting Bold Boundaries

Forgiving was one thing. Setting healthy ongoing boundaries was another.

In some relationships, especially where soul ties and emotional dependencies exist, it can be a long, painful journey to break free of the influence and control of another. This was my experience as I walked with Jesus and let him reveal my brokenness to me.

My ex-wife plagued me with phone calls and degrading verbal assaults. I felt helpless to stop her. Why? When we were married, I had abdicated my power to gain from her the approval I'd never received as a child. In order to receive this approval I gave her the power to dominate and abuse me. While we were married, she had used that power to control me. After we divorced, she used it to torment me with these calls I had no boundaries to stop.

Even after I married Linda, the phone calls from my ex continued, pouring anxiety and confusion into our relationship. I began seeing a counselor for help. He taught me to become indignant at boundary violations and say, "How dare you?"

After I poured out my story, the counselor got straight to the point.

"You need to erase her from the list of people you're trying to get approval from."

I saw it immediately. My need for her approval had allowed the abuse to continue. I was taking anything she wanted to dish out to gain her acceptance. I had no boundaries.

Needing to remove my ex from my approval list became one of the biggest *aha* moments of my life. The chains were about to break.

I realized I could choose to repent of my approval-seeking and go to God for what I needed instead of looking to a woman for it in my brokenness. I could stop worshipping others for the approval I craved instead of worshipping God. My ex—and the endless quest for her approval—had become an idol God wanted to remove from my life.

I feared my ex because I had given her so much power over me. I had made her my addiction. Instead of being a man, I was looking for her approval to make me one.

This is the painful masculine trap of the insecure man who looks to his woman to tell him he has what it takes. Of course, the woman can't tell him this; only God can. When a man abdicates his masculine strength, it's easy for a woman to take advantage of him.

My ex and I were divorced now, but I had not redefined the relationship, nor established healthy boundaries with her. She could still do what she'd always done, what I'd always let her do. When you've been divorced, your ex needs to be reoriented to you with new boundaries. Without them, he or she may seek to control you and interfere in the dynamics of your new marriage. This was my problem.

Now, with this new knowledge, that I had given away my power for her approval, I took away her right of inappropriate access to my heart and emotions. I would no longer let her manipulate me with guilt or her opinions of me. The soul tie needed to be broken.

I chose to no longer care what she thought of me, and I removed her from my emotional database. I took away her power to manipulate me by no longer living for her approval.

The next time she bombarded me with questions, I knew what to do.

"That's none of your business," I said. "We're divorced now. I don't have to answer any more of your questions, so don't ask them."

Her entitled assaults were stopped, and my repentance of idolatry repositioned me in the relationship in a healthy, empowered way. When we don't understand and apply needed boundaries, we violate *ourselves* and open the door for other people to degrade us. The truth is, we live in a fallen, sinful world filled with broken people. Life and relationships are messy. Without healthy boundaries, we can become trapped in toxic partnerships fueled by the brokenness of others and ourselves.

Of course, setting bold boundaries is easier said than done. Here are some actions you may need to take:

- Precipitate a crisis, if necessary, to upset the status quo of an abusive or out-of-control relationship. Rock the boat, or nothing will change. Interrupting the toxic pattern might mean standing up for yourself, removing yourself from the situation, getting counseling for yourself, or calling the police.

- Remove the tormenting influence of a destructive person from your life, unless or until they can behave. The removal is sometimes permanent, involving a restraining order. This might mean hanging up the phone or blocking their number when they violate your boundaries, which includes respectful speech without degrading words, threats, or coercion.

- Refuse to allow another to speak into your life who has forfeited that right through their behavior or actions. If they can't respect you, they lose the privilege of a relationship with you. This means they cannot come over or have access to your home or family members.

- If domestic violence—physical, emotional, or sexual abuse has or might occur, pursue physical separation and get legal backup as needed. Henry Cloud explains it this way: "You have to go into protection mode, not helping mode, when dealing with evil people. You can't reason with evil people, and there are some people whose desire is to hurt and do destructive things.

Evil people are not reasonable. They seek to destroy. So you have to protect yourself—ergo, lawyers, guns, and money. I use that phrase to symbolize resources that you use to protect yourself. Sometimes you must see people for who they truly are, protect yourself, make a very necessary ending, and have nothing more to do with them.[1]

• Learn how to set boundaries to protect yourself from the destructive behaviors of addicted, abusive, or dysfunctional people, including family members. To protect yourself, seek help and counsel from those who are equipped to deal with your situation. Talk to others for help and perspective. Don't withdraw, isolate, and suffer. There is no shame in bringing light and truth into your life.

3. Seek Healing for Your Own Brokenness

What has kept you in a toxic relationship?

Breaking free requires an answer to this question and a willingness to address the brokenness in your life.

Hosea 4:6 says, "My people are destroyed for lack of knowledge.

God never shames or punishes us for what we don't know in this process of self-discovery. He always leads with love, joy, and tenderness. Even when the process is painful as God exposes and heals my heart and mind, I can rest in his loving presence knowing that his desire for me is healing and freedom.

Are you enabling someone?

There is a fine line between showing mercy and enabling an addict or abuser. Counselors can provide safety and guidance, and we need others to help us see what we cannot. It's hard to see clearly what's going on when we are trapped in broken cycles.

Our brokenness can blind us to patterns of relating we may be trapped in. We may think inappropriate behavior from others is normal because that's all we've observed and known. Allowing counselors or mentors into our unhealthy reality can help us see our way to freedom.

Others with experience and wisdom can help us with strategies we can't find on our own. They know how to change the steps by speaking the truth and can help us learn a new dance that is healthy and free.

Has a toxic relationship become your idol?

Because of my upbringing without boundaries, I thought being run over, suppressed, and violated was normal. I had never seen anything else. Nevertheless, the actions of my ex were inappropriate, and I needed to do something to protect myself from her abusive cycles. I saw that I'd created the relational dynamics causing so much pain in my life. I had opened the door to this by making my ex my "god," by seeking her for what only God could give me. I had been chained to an empty well and was still there.

Danny Silk, in his powerful book *Keep Your Love On,* explains,

> We have a deep God-created need for intimacy, love, and comfort. But if we look to things that

were not designed to meet those needs and elevate them above everything else—making them idols—then the result is always bondage and destruction.

It's only when we place God at the center that we can access comfort, peace, safety, joy, and pleasure that truly meets our deepest needs. . . .

Think of a man who makes his wife his god. He makes her responsible for his joy, identity, and comfort—all things only God should satisfy. Inevitably his anxiety goes through the roof whenever he can't control her.

He has put her in charge of such deep needs in his life that he becomes scared of her. She is his addiction. And when he can't get his fix, he's a mess. His only hope is to turn to God. God must satisfy his needs. No one else can do that "God job" like God can.[2]

I think we create suffering when we overvalue the opinions of others. Self-awareness allows us to see what we are doing and make different choices.

CHAPTER FOURTEEN

Celebrate the Gift of Sexuality

It's what we wanted in marriage: to know and be known by another in the safey of unconditional love.

— Barbara Rainey

In chapter 11 we explored how our differences can open the door to greater love and intimacy. The same truth applies to the different attitudes and needs that men and women bring to the topic of sex. The more we understand what is going on in the hearts and minds of our lovers, the more we will enjoy connecting with them emotionally and sexually.

The Longings of Eve

"My lover said to me, 'Rise up, my darling! Come away with me, my fair one!'" (Song 2:10 NLT).

"Pursue me."

Every woman longs to hear the romantic invitation of her lover. Her lover is initiating. He's coming for her and she's responding. Eve was formed out of a rib taken from Adam. A part of him is missing now, and Eve has it. She wants him to come and get it.

Women long to be pursued romantically, not only during courtship but for the rest of their lives. This desire doesn't go away after the honeymoon. As a man, you may feel secure in her love for you, but the question is never completely settled in her heart. Remember the two towers? If she doubts your love for her, she may retreat into her tower where lies about her self-esteem tell her she's not worthy of the pursuit after all. *Maybe I am not enough.*

She needs reassurance from her man.

When I speak of romantic pursuit, I'm not talking about flowers, dinners, and gifts, nice as those are, but rather, his participation in her life. A woman wants him to initiate and pursue her. She yearns to be known, not just sexually but on a soul level.

She longs for him to pursue her heart by joining in her struggles, dreams, and joys. This caring for her heart is the pinnacle of romance for her; it's her relational lifeblood. Romantic pursuit to her is mutuality, doing life *with* her, and sharing in building a corporate kingdom together.

In his book *What Wives Wish Their Husbands Knew about Women,* James Dobson answers this important question from a reader:

> I have often wondered why women seem to need romantic involvement so much more than men. . . . Why are they [men] so uninformed of this common aspect of feminine nature?"[1]

Here is his answer:

> They haven't been told. For centuries women have been admonished to meet their husbands' sexual needs — or else. Every female alive knows that the masculine appetite for sex demands gratification, one way or the other.
>
> What I have been attempting to say is that a woman's need for emotional fulfillment is just as pressing and urgent as the physiological requirement for sexual release in the male. Both can be stymied but at an enormous cost!
>
> As such, it is as unfortunate for a man to ignore his wife's need for romantic love as it is for her to foreclose on his sexual appetite.

So, it seems each is depending on the other to supply something vital they need to be fulfilled. The tension builds because both obtain fulfillment differently. Since we aren't walking in the other's shoes, we don't know how much it means to them.

We both want connection and intimacy but have to cross different bridges to find it. We are pushed to learn to honor the differences and needs of others. This is hard for us since our natural tendency is to demand sameness, rather than take the hard road of growth to learn about and then honor the different needs of our spouse. Our commitment to love enables this. Marriage is more than getting what we need when we want it.

"Explore me."

John Eldredge says in *Captivating*, that "every woman longs for a beauty to unveil. . . ." This is in her heart, part of her design. He explains, "One of the deepest ways a woman bears the image of God is in her mystery. By 'mystery' we don't mean 'forever beyond your knowing,' but 'something to be explored.' "[2]

This sheds light on her desire to connect with him relationally and through conversation. She wants him to "explore her." Not just sexually, but she might think, *Explore the mystery of my soul. Find out about me so I can unveil the beauty, the mystery of myself to you, not just my body.*

It's as if she's asking him, though she won't say it out loud, *I have a beauty to unveil. It's mysterious, not on the surface, and you'll have to come after it to find it. Come away with me! I'm the undiscovered country! Am I worth the adventure to discover me?*

She so longs for the answer to be yes! She hears the yes, and feels pursued, when he searches for her deep heart and connects with her there.

The man's rite of passage is to figure out how to pursue her in a way she can find the love and connection her heart craves.

This romantic pursuit meets an important need for reassurance. I call this a man's rite of passage because a self-centered boy must grow out of his self-focus and narcissism to love a woman properly.

It's not that he's just selfish, she can be selfish too—he just hasn't figured out her heart yet, and how different her needs are than his. He will find in learning to care for her heart that her sexual responsiveness is usually not an issue.

This is a man's relational education and goes much further than knowing how to sexually relate. It involves his assignment of exploring and knowing a woman's heart. This does not come easy for most men.

To him, sex with her is the end game; the other, caring for her heart and needs, is not on his mind at first. Men need the help of their ladies to train them to care for their hearts. Most guys haven't been taught to do this. He probably didn't observe it at home, certainly not from the world, which elevates selfish lust and using women, rather than loving and caring for them. There is nothing tender about selfish sex.

Ladies, he needs your help, respect, and the help of others to succeed. Men tend to isolate, be selfish, seek pleasure, avoid pain and sacrifice, and start the marriage journey with these attitudes. Most women end up disappointed with the attention and focus they receive from their men not long into the marriage. It's not all fairy-tale thinking on her part. It can be a passive man not showing interest in his lady's heart.

Also, ladies, you will need to learn the courage to give your heart away-and learn to respect someone who doesn't understand or know your heart. Your challenge is to learn about his motivations, needs, and thinking too.

His disconnect from you is not a reflection on his intelligence — or that he doesn't care — it's that his wiring is so different that he lacks the grid for what your heart needs. If sex is the focus that meets *his* needs — he has no way of knowing you need more than *just sex*. It helps to remember that God created Adam and Eve differently on purpose. He insists we learn to love and care for each other in our differing needs to feel loved.

When you learn each other's love languages and the different ways you feel loved, you can cultivate intimacy better together. [3] This is learning to love, and it's a lifetime journey, the quest that never stops. We find that it's much more than sex and erotic pleasure, although this is included in the deal.

"Desire me."

In addition to being pursued, women long to be *desired*. As we revealed earlier, the unspoken question she asks him every day is this: *Am I beautiful and worth pursuing?*

Have you noticed that even very beautiful women can wrestle with insecurities about their beauty and worth? Remember this is Eve's painful wound, and lies about her beauty can haunt her. She needs to hear, "You are God's daughter, a princess created in his image, and very lovely! I love you!"

This can be said in many ways, but a husband has special access to his wife's heart and the privilege of reassuring her in ways no other can. It's called romance, and it tells her *I'm worth it.*

This ongoing message of loving reassurance breaks shame off her heart and empowers her to give herself to her husband. This truth of his love and desire for her — of her value to him—needs to be communicated often to bring the reassurance her heart longs for. She needs this to risk giving her heart away to him over and over again.

A woman is hardwired to want to be pursued, explored, and desired. Unveiling her beauty to a man who desires her, pursues her heart, and explores her soul is essential to her femininity. It's easy for a man to miss this. Remember "Mirror, mirror on the wall"? Subconsciously, her husband is now the mirror.

John Eldredge adds that a woman's mystery reflects the image of God, particularly how God longs to be pursued by us. God is "no harlot," John explains, giving himself to just anyone. His mystery must be pursued and valued or it won't be unveiled to us. "This is crucial to any woman's soul, not to mention her sexuality. 'You cannot simply have me. You must seek me, pursue me. I won't let you in unless I know you love me.'"[4]

The Longings of Adam

Earlier, we shared that a man has the same needs as his woman only he tends to receive them differently than she does. Men reach to their wives for affirmation and validation, mostly through sexual union. Women receive affirmation and validation through romantic pursuit, talking, and relational engagement.

"Don't shame me."

In the same way a woman wants to be desired by her husband, a man also needs to be desired by his wife. If she doesn't desire him sexually, it can create an attitude within him that says, *Why even try to connect with her at all, why even bother?*

I felt shamed many years ago by my ex-wife in my first, failed two-year marriage. Sex was not a priority for her, and she was mostly unavailable. It's frustrating and lonely for a man in this situation.

Trauma and past abuse can cause either partner to shut down sexually. An excellent resource for sexual healing, explored at length, is *The Wounded Heart* by Dan Allender.[5] These are painful areas, but God is faithful to bring us on the healing journey to wholeness and joy. There is hope!

"Welcome me sexually."

For a man, affirmation of his manhood is received through his sexuality, specifically through willing and invited intercourse with his wife. Having sex out of a sense of duty is no fun for anyone. Anyone can consent to sex but still not be an enthusiastic participant. As she wilts without his initiative to romance and pursue her, he wilts without her responsiveness. A man loves enthusiasm and engagement—not *Let's get this over with.* Loving engagement by both without holding back makes sex in marriage the most satisfying. A man needs to feel loved and respected as a man, not viewed as an animal with a drive needing to be tamed. In the same way, a woman needs to feel loved as a person rather than an object.

The Response of Eve

Just as a man can neglect his wife by forgetting and forsaking romance, so a woman can neglect him by forgetting and forsaking his sexual needs in the relationship.

Barbara Rainey, in her book with her husband, Dennis Rainey, *Rekindling the Romance*, states,

- Marriage is intended to be redemptive for both men and women. God has given us women the privilege and ability to bring life to our husbands with our love. Women have enormous power with men and we can use it for good and for evil.

- Your power can meet his aloneness and companionship needs, bless his sexual identity, protect him from temptation, and keep him for life.[6]

Barbara reveals that a woman's attitude toward her husband's sexuality is important because she alone has the power to bless him sexually and affirm his male identity.

Your husband needs to feel that when he initiates intimacy with you, you "welcome" him and want to "receive" him. By doing so, you affirm him—indeed you affirm his leadership and initiative, the very essence of his manhood."[7]

Keys to the Celebration

Celebrate by asking for what you need.

While studying this emotional and sexual arena, I see that our needs aren't so different. We're all about the same and feel similar fears and insecurities we're reluctant to talk about.

Perhaps it's our fear of being vulnerable that keeps us from being honest about what we need involving sex. Why do we struggle with openly talking about what we need?

I found a quote in Alex Avila's devotional book that says it well: "The more insight into our patterns and underlying feelings, and the more humble and vulnerable we can become, the greater our capacity for communicating our needs and longings."[8]

As we develop security as a couple, we can be more vulnerable and risk talking openly about sex and the needs and struggles we have. When we feel loved and accepted we can take those risks.

Celebrate each other's communication strategies.

I am more on the emotional, feeling side of personality. My two primary love languages are meaningful touch and quality time.[9] Linda feels more loved by acts of service. I will be frustrated and depressed waiting for her to meet my needs if I think, *She should know what my need is and what I want. She should initiate and make herself available; to talk, make love, or whatever.*

But that's fairy-tale thinking; she won't know what I need unless I tell her and teach her what it looks like. I come up with a creative statement, get her undivided attention, and say, "I feel most loved by you when . . . ," or "When this doesn't happen, I feel empty inside."

Without attacking or putting her down, I must be respectfully assertive and trust her to respond. I could say, "Can you get your schedule out? I want to schedule some quality time together" or "Let's get a date night going tonight."

I won't quit until I get what I need. I don't nag, but I initiate and make it happen. Anyone can do this by being proactive. You must become your partner's teacher when it comes to getting your needs met. They don't know what you want unless you tell them. You have to get in touch with your needs and learn to articulate them. Clear, bold communication is the answer.

I can stay in the victim role, depressed over what I'm not getting, or I can take responsibility for what I need, get empowered, and start initiating, engaging, and talking. Courage won't give up, and if this approach doesn't work, I'll try another or another. Love never fails.

Remember ladies, guys tend to perform and fix rather than feel and understand. You can help them see it's not their performance you need, but their engaged presence. You would rather have him be there to hug you rather than work late at the office to pay the bills. It's up to us, both guys and gals, to build into our marriages the communication to secure what we need.

It helps to show our partner what it would look like if your needs were met. If you want romance, talk to him about what that means to you and would look like. Maybe you need sex every other week, and he's an every-other-day kind of guy, or maybe it's the opposite. Maybe you want a different kind of quality time. What does it look like? There are no set rules. We create what we want and agree together on it.

Linda and I recently had a sex talk. Our relationship is wonderful, and I'm not deprived in our marriage sexually, but was feeling some frustration. I have a choice: I can withdraw and smolder, resent, and blame her for not caring, or I can risk emotional honesty, reveal how I feel, and explore it with her. I don't always ace it, but I won't let my brokenness or unmet need sow distance between us. I will talk to her instead.

No matter how long you've been married, the need for communication about sex and other needs never goes away, and priorities need to change at times to keep our marriages life-giving. This only can happen when we initiate, communicate, and respond.

Celebrate the moment, not the end goal.

I'm not writing a sex manual here but will write this for you while blushing, after all these years of sexual fulfillment with Linda.

You're setting yourself up for stress and frustration if your expectations are too high for the experience of sex itself. You must take performance off sex as a couple and lovingly enjoy each other, letting the experience be what it is.

The honeymoon eventually ends, but sexual fulfillment doesn't have to.

Edwin Louis Cole, author of *Maximized Manhood*, said many years ago at a Promise Keepers rally, "Old people stop having babies, they don't stop having sex." Your biorhythms change through the seasons of life. You find you aren't a teenager anymore. Accept where you both are through these seasons. You are setting yourself up for a sense of failure if you expect the ultimate peak experience for both of you in each sexual encounter.

Ed Wheat, in his book *Love Life for Every Married Couple*, explains,

> When couples strive to obtain an orgasm without regard to enjoying their time together, sex becomes work rather than pleasure . . . Women tell me that they do not always need or desire an orgasm during sexual encounters, but their husbands cannot understand this and feel like failures unless an orgasm occurs. . . .
>
> So husband, if you want to build love in your marriage . . . Concentrate on pleasing your wife rather than anxiously pushing her towards a sexual release. If she thinks you are pressuring her, she will begin to dread the possibility of failure rather than relaxing and surrendering to her own physical response.[10]

"Respect me."

The love languages of most guys are words of affirmation and meaningful touch. If she doesn't respect him, but criticizes him, and withholds sex from him, it's a double emasculation to him. She is only not meeting his need for sex but his need to be respected and affirmed. Women may not realize how vulnerable he is and how much this weakens the marriage.

I'm not talking about situations where abuse or infidelity are involved. Rather, I'm referring to a lack of respect shown because a wife doesn't think her husband is meeting up to the standard she believes he should. The most powerful thing a spouse can do is brag to his or her friends about their spouse. Likewise, the most destructive thing a spouse can do is roast their loser husband or wife in front of friends (Prov. 14:1; Eph. 5:33). Who knows how many divorces have been hatched here—by gaining the negative agreement, then support to leave the *bad spouse*.

Celebrate your differences

We can celebrate the gift of our sexuality better by understanding and honoring our sexual differences. This happens when we explore, understand, and validate these differences. We've talked a lot about differences in this book, and these matter in the bedroom.

Difference in sex drive

It's no secret that men have a reputation for being more sexually driven than women. This can create the tension that he's always after her, and she's always running from him. She can play "catch me if you can," but she has to let him catch her sometimes or it's no fun. Barbara Rainey says,

> As you probably have experienced, these radical differences in approach to romance set the stage for repeated clashes in marriage—the husband pursues romance based on his sexual passion, and the wife goes after relationship.[11]

As a new marriage inevitably polarizes, the couple is pushed to learn how to cope with their different needs and sexual realities. He can be sensitive to her sexually, by not overlooking her other pressing relational needs. She can affirm him by meeting his pressing physical needs. Happiness can be found in their love dance as they learn to understand and satisfy one another.

Stimulated differently

"Women are stimulated more by touch and romantic words. They are far more attracted to a man's personality, while men are stimulated by sight."[12]

She typically needs more time with lovemaking than he does, and he needs to honor her lovingly in her experience by being patient and unselfish.

Advance notice and consideration help her. Some women have revealed they like advance notice and enjoy anticipating sexual time together. Guys tend to be more spontaneous and are always anticipating possibilities. Talk about this and have fun with it so you can enjoy sex together.

Sexual availability and participation

We've shown how women want to be pursued and explored. This helps her feel secure, valued, and honored. Then she can find fulfillment when she unveils her beauty, believing she's loved as a person and not an object.

A man wants to be welcomed and respected when he initiates. He finds safety and security in this. He has the strength to give, and can, when he feels welcomed, validated, and affirmed. This is God's design for the union of a male and a female.

Smalley observes the differences between men and women when approaching sex or making love:

While a man needs little or no preparation for the bedroom, a woman needs to be emotionally and mentally prepared, often hours in advance. Her preparation requires tender consideration, while harshness or abusive treatment can easily remove her desire for days at a time.

When a woman's emotions have been trampled by her husband, she can almost be repulsed by his advances. Many women have told me they feel like prostitutes when they're forced to make love while feeling resentment toward their husbands. However, a man may have NO idea what he is putting his wife through when he does this.[13]

Sex can be a goal-oriented event to the man, but to a woman, it's a continuation of how the relationship is going. She can't turn off her feelings and offenses like a man seemingly can.

She is more connected to her emotions in all areas of living. The more a man understands the heart of a woman and what sex means to her, the more he can bring the care and nurture her heart longs for from him. This is what awakens responsiveness in her.

CHAPTER FIFTEEN

Be a Freedom Fighter

Conflict is the price smart couples pay for a deepening sense of intimacy.

— Les & Leslie Parrott

As we near the end of the book, I want to have a last conversation about conflict. You may have noticed in redemptive conflict that God is behind our conflicts — not the devil. I named this chapter "Be a Freedom Fighter" because our fights come to help us find freedom.

We've spoken of conflict as the plow of God, that he sends it into the ground of our marriage to break up relational patterns that are not life-giving. When there is no conflict or effort to resolve our differences, then there is no spark or growth into intimacy. We end up being uncultivated like a fallow field. Sure we seem to get along, but we live shallow lives together, not connected heart to heart, often seeking the meeting of our needs outside the marriage as we grow apart. Once we see that God is *in* our conflicts, we can cooperate with him in the process of our self-discovery and transformation.

Our relational DNA is discovered through our conflicts. This DNA is the relational blend of our unique personalities, fight styles, and relational operating systems we all have. It helps to see that we fight about the needs and fears flowing from our broken places.

This makes conflict positive as we uncover the wounds God seeks to heal. We can only grow, heal, and win as we learn and embrace these truths. Our growth timeline largely depends on our willingness to humble ourselves and cooperate. This means we can struggle for long periods over issues if we remain proud and stubborn. It also means we can resolve quickly, and move into the joy and connection we desire.

What Is at the Root of the Conflict?

It helps to see that the conflict isn't the problem but the *symptoms* of the problem. The problem behind most fights is our fear and unmet needs. We're afraid of losing, or we need something we're not getting. The only way to find that need or fear is to fight about it. We can't find intimacy blockers without dragging them out and fighting over them. God helps us here by targeting these blockers for us with his state-of-the-art targeting system.

When we can take our focus off our partner, and observe our inner reactions, we can see what we're fighting about.

Think about it: What makes you scared? What is your most pressing need?

If we keep those questions in mind it speeds up the process of finding the root of the fight. When conflict starts, at first you may have no idea what's going on. It hurts. You often think your partner is just being selfish and resisting you, so you go into attack mode, and it's game on. Usually, your security or freedom is threatened, or you fear you won't get a felt need met, so you resist and dig in.

We don't know we are both hurting and afraid and that the two towers are close by. When we learn to fight fairly, we'll spend less time in our towers and more time enjoying connection and intimacy we never thought possible.

As we answer God's call to self-awareness, we can understand our dynamics and discern the emotional currents running under the surface of our relationship. When we can see what's going on, knowledge gives us the power to use wisdom in these sensitive dynamics.

Identify the fear and bring assurance— meet that need— and the conflict will be resolved. It may sound simplistic, but when you drill down to understand what's going on, the doors to communication and understanding open up, and you have a strategy to talk about. Needs and fears are validated and honored. Think of your fight as a knot in a shoelace. It just takes a little time and effort to get it free—you just can't give up.

For example, you may think you're fighting about money and overspending when the underlying issue is security. And a conflict you think is regarding in-laws, might at its root be about loyalty. Sometimes more than one need can fuel the same conflict.

It's helpful when we see what our needs and fears are doing. Let's see how we can identify the root of different examples of conflict and move toward resolution.

1. Identify the need that's fueling the conflict.

What are the common unmet needs fueling most conflicts? According to Tim and Joy Downs in *The Seven Conflicts*, they fall into the following categories:[1]

These are the seven conflicts: security, loyalty, responsibility, caring, order, openness, and connection.

Security: Protection and Provision

The security conflict is over the need to feel safe, provided for, and reassured. This goes deeper than just money and being provided for, especially for ladies. A woman needs openness and honesty from her man as well. When he lets her into his heart, she feels safer and can trust him more.

According to Willard Harley in *His Needs, Her Needs*, "A sense of security is the bright golden thread woven through all of a woman's five basic needs. If a husband does not maintain honest and open communication with his wife, he undermines her trust and eventually destroys her sense of security."[2]

Men want their wives to trust them, but women can only trust their husbands if they meet their security needs. Security conflicts are likely greater among ladies since her need for security is woven through all of her five basic needs.

She needs security at a deep level and reaches out to him for it. It helps when guys gain an awareness of this and try to provide the honesty and openness gals need to feel secure. The more a man can reassure his wife and make her feel secure, the happier they will be. Men need to be intentional in opening their hearts to their wives to understand their security needs.

Men, this looks like not keeping secrets from her, and showing emotional vulnerability by giving her access to your feelings and emotions. How can she trust you if you won't give her this? Without access she has no idea whether you love her or not—your heart is not available to her. If you aren't giving it to her, then she's not sure who's getting it, and can grow insecure.

When a spouse chooses a course of action that threatens their partner's need for security, conflict is inevitable. For instance, one person may feel more secure by saving for the future, while his or her spouse wants to spend money on a cruise or buy a lake house. There is usually a saver and a spender in a marriage. A conflict that seems to be about spending is being fueled by a deeper need for security. If the couple tries to resolve the conflict by arguing about money without seeing the deeper need for financial security, they won't succeed.

In some cases, both spouses may have the same need but are attempting to meet it in different ways. For example, one person may want to install an alarm system on the house, while the other deems it an unnecessary expense. The person who wants the alarm system is likely expressing a need for physical security.

The spouse who doesn't want the alarm may also have an unmet need for security, in this case, financial. If the debate stays focused on the pros and cons of alarms, they are missing an opportunity to explore what really matters to them—i.e., how they feel about money and the security it represents. We need to look deeper than the surface thing we're fighting about to see the need or fear underneath to resolve. When the need is seen and identified, we can then talk about it and honor and validate. Until we are talking about and validating the need itself, we will go in circles around the real issue.

Loyalty: Faithfulness and Priority

Your spouse needs to know without a doubt that they are first on your priority list. You choose them above all others, and you desire to honor their needs first. When they feel bumped from that slot, conflict will arise.

You may think your spouse is being petty when conflict arises about time spent away from them, or when you choose other things and pastimes instead of being with them. The fight isn't about your choice; it's about loyalty and security. *Will you choose me? Am I really number one?* They wonder.

Responsibility: Obligation and Expectation

The responsibility conflict is about rules and what you should or shouldn't do. It's about what you're obligated or expected to do. One spouse seems to be more responsible than the other in most marriages. The responsible one will then push the other to be as responsible as they are and disapprove if they don't live up to their standard.

Examples of obligation and expectation being imposed could include,

- He wants to work thirty hours a week, and she wants him to work more hours.
- "We need to get those weeds treated and the lawn mowed, what will the neighbors think?"
- "I feel embarrassed that we're always late for church."

The conflict isn't about the circumstances, it's about responsibility, what we should be doing, and what's expected of us. It's about how we put pressure on each other.

Obligations and expectations need to be talked about, honored, and negotiated for the conflict to be resolved.

Caring: Awareness and Initiative

The caring conflict shows up when one or both spouses feel neglected in the marriage. The underlying need is generally feeling not supported, nurtured, or cared for. Affection and romance are often at the root of a caring conflict. Lack of quality time or conversation can fuel this conflict. These examples explain it and reveal the disconnect:

- "They aren't tuned in to me or care about my problems."
- "They aren't available to me when I need them."
- "If they cared, there would be some romance, sex, or affection."
- "He sees how much I'm dealing with; why doesn't he pitch in?"
- "Why is she unwilling to enter into my struggle?"
- "Why can't she affirm me or appreciate how hard I work?"

Order: Structure and Control

Structure says, "There's a plan for everything." Conflict can arise in this for an unstructured personality. To them, too much order can seem stifling and destroy feelings of spontaneity or freedom.

- "Why do we need to schedule and plan every minute?"
- "I burn out if we plan too much. Can't we just relax and let the day evolve?"
- "We don't need reservations; if we can't get in, we'll try somewhere else."
- "I feel more comfortable if we plan and schedule everything out ahead of time."
- "We can't just get on the plane and fly; we need tickets and timelines."
- "Can we organize the closet and the garage so everything isn't so chaotic?"
- "I'm not lost, we'll find it, I don't need to ask for directions."

As fate would have it, there seems to be a planner and an unstructured spouse in every marriage. It helps to remember that God did this and we need each other. Without a planner we can't imagine the chaos — we'd all be beach bums, late, and there wouldn't be any shore excursions. Without the unstructured, there wouldn't be much spontaneity and surely not as much fun!

Openness: Sociability and Energy

This conflict is about how the party animal and the introvert stay married. Parties energize the extrovert while they can be draining to one who enjoys solitude. The need to stay energized fuels this conflict. Replenishers and depleters—the things that refill you or drain you—need to be negotiated and agreed upon. You will find a list for those in the study guide at the end of the book.

One might say, "Do we have to have someone over again this weekend? Can't it be just us two for a change?"

And the other responds, "You are such a stick in the mud. You never want to do anything."

"I don't mind doing things and having people over, but some quality time with just you is important to me. Couldn't we schedule both?"

"There is a good concert coming up. Why don't we plan a date night?" or "Can't we stay home this weekend and do stuff around here instead of going to the mountains again?"

Connection: Communication and Decision-Making

The inability to connect, agree, and decide together fuels this conflict. Different styles must be worked through to connect, honor, and find agreement.

"I wish she wouldn't talk in circles, but just get to the point so we could resolve this."

"I can't think as fast as he does, and need more time to get in touch."

"I wish he wouldn't get frustrated and withdraw so quickly, but instead stay engaged so we could get somewhere."

"If he cared, he would try to understand my feelings instead of trying to fix everything."

"Why can't she just listen to me without jumping to conclusions?"

2. Explore the need in a safe environment.

Once we identify the need that is fueling our conflict, we then explore it in the context of safety. We do this in our secure castle. Exploring means the ability to discuss what's going on without defensiveness, judgment, or attack. This is challenging when things heat up and emotions, wounds, and fears want to take over.

It means curbing our emotions and using the Rules of Engagement to stop escalation. Also, the Speaker-Listener in the study guide tool makes sure we can hear and understand each other. It means forsaking power to win and trying instead to understand each other at a deeper level.

To do this, you'll need to use words that don't demand or push, but instead convey an attitude that welcomes and invites. The right talking style and attitude will keep us from sabotaging the process.

"I want to understand you and find agreement together about this. Can we talk about it?"

"Can we go deeper and find the need that's behind this conflict?"

"We can do this! Let's use the speaker-listener exercise to understand what each of us is saying to the other."

3. Validate the need and the feelings involved.

All feelings must be heard, honored, and validated to resolve a conflict. If we don't accept the emotions our partner is experiencing, they will not be emotionally honest with us.

Again, use words that don't demand or push but instead welcome and invite. Consider this dialogue between two spouses:

"What are you feeling now? You seem agitated."

"I feel hurt and angry."

"I hear you saying you feel hurt and angry. Can you tell me more about that?

"No. You'll just tell me I'm being emotional."

"Can you give me a chance to understand you so I can validate your struggle? I love and care about you and want to understand your needs so I can meet them. What do you need from me that I'm not giving you? Can we explore this together? I don't want you hurt."

4. Identify a strategy for resolution.

You've identified each other's needs and validated each other's emotions. Now it's time for resolution. Now that you understand what matters to each of you, is there a way forward that meets both of your needs?

Come up with a strategy to resolve the current conflict, but don't stop there. Talk about what you can do the next time there's a conflict. All through our marriage, we've done what we call postmortems on our conflicts. We ask ourselves questions like, "What just happened?" Then we unpack it, look at it, and ask, "How can we handle it differently next time?" and "The next time we clash, what's our strategy?" By doing this, we dismantle the energy of repeating patterns. We are determined not to be victims of what we keep doing to each other.

Case Study: The Crowded House

I asked Linda recently if she could remember a loyalty conflict we've had. She brought up her first visit to my parents' home at Christmas. The house was packed with eight kids, some grandkids, and two parents. It was traumatic for her to experience the cultural clash between our two families.

She has one younger sister, and their home life was more structured and less chaotic than mine. I have seven brothers and sisters, and the dynamics in our home were unstructured, emotional, and loud. I was used to this emotional swimming pool and liked it.

I made a *Meet the Parents* mistake early on at her parents' house at the dinner table. Her father was talking, and I interrupted. He looked at me offended like I had spit on the table or worse. I felt red-faced and ashamed as I soon learned the "house rules" around *not* interrupting, part of their family's "speaking etiquette." It was way too uptight for me. I felt suppressed.

Growing up, my family couldn't have been more opposite. The words unstructured and free-for-all would best describe us. Everyone talked at once, and if someone else was talking, you simply raised your volume so *you* could be heard above the din. No one listened to each other.

You can imagine how unsettling a first-time week-long visit at Christmastime was for Linda.

As soon as we got there, I jumped back into the normal relational dynamics of my family upbringing. Leaving Linda in the kitchen with strangers talking over each other and bouncing around, I left with my oldest brother to catch up, thinking nothing about it.

That night when we retired to the guest room, the argument began. Linda told me she felt "abandoned and thrown to the wolves," adding, "When you're around your brother Jack, it's like I drop off the face of the earth. You're completely inattentive to me."

I thought *You've got to be kidding me! You're jealous of my brother? You have me all the time! I finally get a chance to see my family, and you want me to sit with you and hold your hand?*

I was smart enough not to say these words out loud, but that's what I was thinking.

Her needs? I guess I assumed those were supposed to go away when it came time to be with my family. I was learning that new environments expose new needs.

She continued accusing, "All day you left me abandoned and on my own, in an environment I didn't understand."

I felt perplexed, confused, and helpless. The truth was I hadn't given a thought to how she would respond to my family. I guess I figured she would just fit in and find her way. Isn't that how it worked? I hadn't anticipated a special needs deal I would have to unpack.

I was unprepared for her reaction. I felt rejected by her and a little desperate at losing my sibling relationships to this clingy, insecure person I had married. I had never seen this side of her, as she had never seen this side of my family. I thought, *How much is it going to take to meet this need? Were we going to need to just pack up and leave because she couldn't handle my family? How were we going to get past this?*

Here's what we did.

Step 1: Identified the Need

The more we talked, I realized several unmet needs for Linda were fueling her emotions. Feeling I was choosing my family over her, she had an unmet loyalty need for me to make her a priority. She also needed to feel connected to me during our visit in order to feel safe and secure.

I hadn't seen these needs in her before, so they hadn't registered with me. Besides, I had been too busy sliding into old family dynamics that felt comfortable and fun to me. My preference was to embrace the default patterns in my family, so her needs — once expressed to me — left me stunned.

Step 2: Explored the Conflict in a Safe Environment

I admit as Linda and I began to unpack her emotions and needs, I didn't immediately create a safe environment for us. I was surprised at her reaction to me with my family. It sounded like she thought I was some uncaged animal and that she saw all my family members that way.

My first emotional response was anger, confusion, and accusation as I told myself, *She's just being selfish!*

This conflict resolution stuff was new to me, uncomfortable, and hard to do. Thinking about what I would have to do to honor her feelings made me feel restricted, and afraid I would lose my freedom.

A question pressed hard on my heart: *Who is more important here, her or them?* And I hated the choice. It felt like I was betraying my family and giving up something that belonged to me.

In reality, it was a healthy and appropriate boundary. It was a "leaving and cleaving" adjustment that God was making in me. It was hard but necessary as I learned to grow in love and honor my wife's needs and feelings above my desires and rights.

What really mattered, getting my way or honoring and protecting her? (Eph. 5:28–33).

Step 3: Validated the Feelings Involved

I realized if I was going to meet these needs in Linda, I would have to better understand her feelings about "who I became" when I was around my family. How she felt was, well, how she felt. Those emotions weren't right or wrong. I needed to understand and accept them.

I started carefully using phrases like this: "So, you're saying . . ."

"Yes, that's how I feel."

"And when I do that, you feel this?"

"Yes, that's what I feel."

I had to process and honor the way she felt about my family without getting defensive and siding with them against her. I couldn't judge or censor her. The resolution to this conflict would be stalled if I became defensive and adversarial. I wanted it to go away as soon as possible.

Step 4: Strategized a Solution

We agreed I would check in with her from time to time to make sure she was okay (i.e., feeling secure). I would bring reassurance.

This met her need by helping her feel I was keeping her at the top of my list and not abandoning her for other people I loved. I checked in a lot at first so she would feel, as she said, "tethered to me and not just floating out there in the chaos." I chose to put her before my family, and in doing so, we were able to develop a corporate identity as we related to them.

I demonstrated faithfulness by submitting myself and being accountable to her. I would only disappear conditionally, for shorter periods so she could feel safe and secure.

God blessed my choosing to honor her in this. I could still participate with my family while covering her so she felt secure in my commitment to her as she integrated into my family of origin.

This conflict dissolved after the first big revelation of how she felt about my family. The check-in was all she needed until she felt more secure. She needed to know she had my loyalty and that *we* were my priority now.

Why Conflict Is Your Friend

View conflict as your friend and not your enemy. Conflict, when used to reveal and resolve unmet needs, is your doorway to greater intimacy. If you see it as a friend knocking at the door and bringing you a marriage gift, you both will be more receptive to it.

Unmet needs can hide just under the surface of a relationship, creating distance and challenges with no obvious source. Conflict reveals these unmet needs with an opportunity to explore and resolve them. In other words, your marriage is better off with it than without it. What a radical statement, but it's true!

Remember these truths:

- Conflict isn't the enemy. It's not from the devil.
- It's an opportunity to draw closer to our spouses and God.
- God is involved and waiting to help us — invite God into each conflict. Together, ask for his wisdom as you begin to identify, explore, and resolve.

I pray God will bring you deeper than you've ever been in intimacy together as you learn to connect over your conflicts.

CHAPTER SIXTEEN

The Road Home

And so — together — they built a life they loved.

— Anonymous

You Have the Power to Make Your Marriage Thrive and Endure

When God made us co-creators with him, he gave us the power to build a good marriage.

"Therefore a man shall leave his father and mother and be joined to his wife, and they shall become one flesh" (Gen. 2:24).

Throughout this book, we've said we possess the power to determine what kind of marriage we will have. We aren't victims of bad marriages. We shape our marriage by the choices we make daily, the dynamics we create, and the kind of growth we are willing to embrace by putting off the old and putting on the new

When we say, "I do," marriage becomes the vehicle for our growth into a one-flesh union. Yes, our initial experience is determined by the immaturity and baggage we've both hauled in with us. But this is transformed in God's presence as we grow, risk, explore, and surrender. We are on the path to loving more maturely and effectively.

You Can Find the Road Home

We feel the joy of oneness when we do the work to become mutually submitted. We are committed to resolving our conflicts. Otherwise, we stay locked in our towers engaged in the power struggle.

Marriage is not two independent personalities living for themselves retaining their private kingdoms. This is the world's model that includes no-risk living and relating. When we marry, we surrender our selfish right to live for ourselves and choose to live, and sacrifice for another. Unselfish living and self-sacrifice show that you've found the road home. It's a process of becoming. It's not like one morning we wake up and have mutuality, but it's a lifelong journey.

Become One by Following These Steps

Here's a reminder of the principles that will keep us on the road home.

1. Stay corporate.

The journey of marriage is for two people to merge their lives and create a new life together. This joining doesn't mean we lose our identity or sense of self. Rather, it's the rich experience of intimately including another soul in our life. We are companions now with a corporate identity. We draw life and nurture from our connection together. It's by laying ourselves down for one another that our lives are merged and raised as one. We know that our two hearts becoming one is a powerful mystery worth pressing into!

It isn't that one can't do something without the other, but it's the exception rather than the rule. When we're apart, we can't wait till we're together again. We didn't marry to be alone but to be together, and our choices reflect that. We're best friends and we want to spend time together.

2. Agree on core values.

Mutual core values will keep you on the road home because they determine your individual and shared goals for your relationship. Shared core values are the riverbanks that channel the direction and quality of your relationship. Unified desires drive your relationship. Your energy follows your desire. Where your treasure is, your heart will follow.

3. Fight fair to Resolve issues.

Unresolved issues keep us from connecting heart to heart. Couples who value oneness are committed to resolving the issues keeping them disconnected. We can be different if we are loving and not dishonoring or degrading.

We are also committed to fighting fair. Oneness is never served when we attack or manipulate, so we agree to fight truthfully and honestly with integrity. Be kind to each other, validate feelings, and prioritize each other's needs.

4. Uplift each other by being positive.

Lovers support one another, talk about their struggles and failures, and call forth character and faith in one another. Don't let negative attitudes and spirits dominate your marriage. Cynicism and complaining come from victims, but you are not victims, you are lovers. If there's a problem, solve it; refuse to complain about it, and it will lose its power to pull you down.

5. Keep short accounts!

We keep short accounts when we pay our emotional bills. This frees us from becoming bitter and punishing emotionally with our words and attitudes. This means we confess, forgive, and clear the air when there has been an offense, a wound, or hurt feelings. We forgive from the heart and mean it. We forgive "lest Satan should take advantage of us; for we are not ignorant of his devices" (2 Cor. 2:10-11).

6. Stay in agreement.

Mutually submit to each other in decision-making. We won't move forward without agreement and a sense of peace that God is with us on our decision. When we decide our course together, God's authority is with us and he empowers us. We balance one another in a complementary way.

7. Enter the emotion pool of the marriage.

We enter into the emotion pool of marriage when we tune in to what our partner is feeling. Ask, "What are you feeling? You seem kind of down." This is a non-threatening style of talking that invites intimacy and connection. Show empathy by asking inviting questions to draw them out. "Tell me more about that." Listen to each other as you articulate struggles and validate their emotions. Talk about strategies to solve a problem. Reminding each other,

"I am with you in this together; you aren't alone."

Inheriting the Kingdom

Love "bears all things, believes all things, hopes all things, endures all things. Love never fails" (1 Cor. 13:7–8).

Couples who stay together for life figure out a way to make it work. They never stop caring and loving until the end. Each spouse learns how to become unselfish. They don't bail out or give up—they overcome brokenness, despair, and regret. They learn to laugh and live joyfully.

They fight their battles and kill the dragons that seek to disconnect them. They are secure in their identity. They lay down their power, and live mutually submitted.

Happily ever after doesn't mean we're always happy. The fairy-tale model breaks down as we face reality. The absence of struggle or negative emotion isn't guaranteed. Truth be told, the road home includes some painful times because marriage doesn't promise a pass from the negative, painful realities of life. Success is overcoming these things together, as unified lovers bound to a covenant under God.

We are gifts to each other to free us from the prisons in our hearts and minds. This is the road home—fighting for each other's hearts and the connection we long for.

In the end, happily ever after isn't magic. It's not luck. It's hard work. It's the ongoing, everyday choices we make to care for one another until the end.

We grow through a lifetime, one day at a time, as God pours His grace out upon us. For those of you on the quest, we pray that you will enjoy your happily ever after.

Study Guide for the Quest

The questions and exercises in this section are designed to help us talk about our relationship. They are purposefully crafted to push you deeper into your heart than you would normally go. Honest talk about what we feel about our spouse is what connects us.

It may help to start a notebook to record your answers and thoughts about these questions. A healing process journal may be helpful. Our ability to process our marriage together is the key to feeling connected — where intimacy is found.

Chapter 1: Someday My Prince Will Come

Connection Questions

1. Can you relate to Danielle's "Someday my prince will come" sign? Unfulfilled expectations hurt, and painful emotions are involved when our dreams of *what could be* don't come true. Can you and your partner talk about what you expected together without being defensive?

2. Talk about how you feel in this season of marriage. Some of our fairy tale thinking may need to be adjusted. We just need to be honest.

Chapter 2: Life in Separate Towers

Connection Questions

1. Tell each other how you feel about *being enough* and having what it takes to be the man or woman you feel you want to be for each other.
2. Confess your fears about your role and what's expected to fill it as the beauty or the knight. Affirm one another with the truth you see about your partner that maybe they can't see.
3. Take turns and share what reassures you. When do you most feel loved and secure with your partner? What would it look like to you? Here are examples of things you could say.

   - "I feel the most loved by you when,
   - "You enter my struggles with me, and I don't feel alone."
   - "You put me first and give me the time I need to feel valued."
   - "You tell me what your feelings and thoughts are."
   - "You are sexually available to me and don't withhold yourself from me."

Chapter 3: The Curse of Stolen Identity

Connection Questions

1. How do you feel about your spouse being the mirror to reflect your true self to you? Do you trust them, or are you afraid?

2. How about accepting God's invitation to let your marriage transform you? Are you in?

3. Can you see where you look to your spouse for more than they can be or give?

4. Can you see where you manipulate and pressure them and turn from that—and ask God to help you find freedom?

State of the Union Evaluation

Take the State of the Union Evaluation separately, then share your thoughts and insights. Answering the following questions will help you identify your honest feelings about yourself, your spouse, and your marriage. Until we can understand and process how we honestly feel about our marriage, we can't manage our feelings truthfully together to move to a more connected place. Select each of the following statements that best describe where *you* are in your relationship now. Check or circle as many as apply. Be honest.

Remember, this is the state of your union—as you see it, feel it, and experience it. There is no right or wrong. The survey is to help you both discover how safe you feel to talk about your honest feelings with each other. If your partner's answers reveal that they don't always feel safe sharing things with you, be careful not to reinforce those feelings by arguing with them or expressing anger. We have had couples who confessed that they made their spouse change their answers!

Start today by creating a safe environment to talk about this survey.

1. I feel cared for and nurtured in this relationship. Circle the best answer and explain why you answered this way.

A little   A lot   Not at all   I need more

2. How safe do you feel opening up to your partner? Circle the best answer and explain why.

Very safe   A little safe   Not safe at all   I feel threatened

3. How would you rate your communication level right now? Circle the best answer and explain why.

Excellent   Good   Fair   Poor   Really bad

4. List the biggest roadblocks to your communication.

5. I feel checked out right now, but I'm willing to work on it. List ways you will work on it. For example—I will talk about where we are and re-engage the process.

6. Circle the dominant emotion(s) you feel with your marriage right now. Tell me why you feel it.

Joy   Excitement   Anger   Love   Hope   Disappointment
Sadness   Frustration   Hurt   Bitterness   Hopelessness
Discouragement

7. I feel honored in our relationship right now. Circle the best answer and explain why.

A little   A lot   Not at all   I need more

8. My needs for intimacy are not met. Circle the best answer and explain why. What would it look like if they were?

A little   A lot   Not at all   I need more

9. I feel like I'm being heard and understood. Circle the best answer and explain why.

A little   A lot   Not at all   I need more

10. I feel lonely, abandoned, or isolated even in my marriage. Circle the best answer and explain why. What could change this?

A little   A lot   Not at all   I need more

11. When I talk, my feelings are validated, or my opinions are honored. Circle the best answer and explain why you feel this way?

A little   A lot   Not at all   I need more

12. Circle the number of your marital satisfaction now from 1 to 10?

1   2   3   4   5   6   7   8   9   10

Least satisfied   Most satisfied

13. Circle the number you think your partner will choose.

1	2	3	4	5	6	7	8	9	10

Least satisfied   Most satisfied

Share your answers and develop a strategy for what you will work on.

14. How well are you communicating right now?

1	2	3	4	5	6	7	8	9	10

Least satisfied   Most satisfied

15. When you do talk, is the outcome usually positive or negative? Explain.

16. How will you rate your emotional honesty level right now? Rate from 1 to 10.

1	2	3	4	5	6	7	8	9	10

Least satisfied   Most satisfied

17. Name an unresolved issue you need to get past to move ahead in your marriage. Tell what it would look like for it to be resolved. Who would do what?

Chapter 4: Invite the Hero of Your Story into Your Quest

Connection Questions

Remember Paul's words? "When I was a child, I spoke as a child, I understood as a child, I thought as a child; but when I became a man, I put away childish things" (1 Cor. 13:11)

Putting away childish things takes a desire to grow and a choice to yield to what God wants to transform in *you*. Our surrender opens the door to what we long for—an ability to love deeply.

1. Tell your spouse where you are on your commitment to putting away childish things.
2. What one thing do you want to work on to be more loving? Tell each other.
3. What did you learn about redemptive conflict in this chapter? Which of the false myths about conflict do you believe that you are going to change?
4. Pray together and invite the Hero of your story into your quest.

Chapter 5: Secure the Castle

Connection Questions

1. How secure do you feel in your covenant? Do you fear your partner may abandon you? Do you ever threaten with divorce? Talk about this and how you feel about the security of your castle.

2. Talk about the Rules of Engagement together and how you can make it safer to talk to each other about conflict. Pick one or two of the rules you may use to blow up a communication bridge and commit to work on those rules together.

Rules of Engagement Covenant

(Print two copies of this covenant; you can also find it at www.dflilly.com.)

I will honor you with my communication.

I will not raise my voice toward you in anger or frustration.

I will not accuse you but will take responsibility for my feelings.

I will not call you names or curse you in any way.

I will not put you down or make negative comparisons.

I will not use condescending words or comments.

I will accept your feelings without invalidating them.

I will not use sarcasm or belittle you.

I will not bully you or intimidate you to get my way.

I will not use guilt to manipulate you.

I will not use sexuality as a power tool to manipulate or control.

I will not blame you for a problem or issue but will work it out with you.

I will listen without interrupting or defending myself when you are talking to me.

I will not fight in the past by bringing up past hurts, or incidents.

I will listen to your needs and will seek to understand you.

If I break any of these rules, you have my permission to stop the conversation until I can keep the rules.

By signing this covenant, I agree to keep the rules that are listed. I make this commitment to my partner and myself and agree to the consequences if I violate the rules. I understand that these rules are to protect our relationship and that they give us the structure we need to have a safe and honoring relationship.

Signature _____

Date: _____

Chapter 6: Win the Power Challenge

Connection Questions

1. Do you recognize the power struggle in your marriage? Who is dominant?
2. How can you level your playing field?
3. Does one of you need to speak up more and be more assertive about things?
4. Do you fear conflict and avoid it? Or do you take the field in conflict?

Chapter 7: Break the Curse of Me Over We

Connection Questions

1. Where do you see the fear that has caused you to control your marriage?
2. Talk about mutuality and if you feel equally honored in decision-making. Does your opinion feel valued?
3. How emotionally safe do you feel with your spouse? Confess any fear you have with them, and what would make you feel safer with them.
4. How do you do in truth-telling? Do you need to take more risks?

From Battleground to Safe Space —
The Speaker-Listener Exercise

"A gentle answer deflects anger, but harsh words make tempers flare" (Prov. 15:1 NLT).

When I read this proverb recently, I was reminded how I am one-half of every conversation I have. What I say and how I say it means everything to my relational dynamics. I can choose where the conversation goes and diffuse escalation or jump on the merry-go-round for the same old ride that stops us in our tracks and sends us to the towers. There we experience lonely frustration and unanswered questions, *Why does it have to be this way? What is it that keeps us from not being able to connect and get past this same old roadblock?*

Couples who escalate are just two people who aren't listening to each other. Both are either trying to win, defend, justify, convince the other, or make a point. Escalation, the enemy of conflict resolution, happens when heated emotions take over. You know the feeling when you pass the point of no return in the process. You stop loving and listening and start defending and fighting. Hurtful words are used, and you punish and attack weak places in your partner to win.

The beauty of the speaker-listener exercise is that it forces you to listen.

When we first start developing our communication skills, we need to be "forced" to listen because we don't listen well. We're too busy defending and forming our rebuttal. We can't defend ourselves and listen at the same time. Listening starts only when defending ends. You can't succeed without structure, and this tool brings that.

You Have the Floor and the Microphone

The way this works in the speaker-listener exercise is one person talks at a time. The speaker has the floor. When we learned this tool, it changed our ability to communicate and honor feelings. We were given a plastic square which was painted with tiles. Whoever held this piece of plastic had the "floor." Only the person who had the floor was able to speak. Finally! One of us could talk without being interrupted and experience the joy of being heard and validated. This created the structure to develop our communication skills.

It's a discipline that exposes how much we feel the need to interrupt or clarify (just to be sure we are understood).

Active listening is hard to do because we are usually forming our rebuttal to what they are saying rather than listening to them. We are defending rather than caring about their feelings. This structure helps train us for this.

Gaining Understanding One Small Bite at a Time

To eat a steak, you must cut it into small pieces. The speaker who has the floor begins sharing whatever they want with the listener who must listen. The listener then must be prepared to rephrase to the speaker what they just told them. The speaker needs to limit their words to a few sentences, or the listener won't be able to remember it all. Let's look at an example.

- SPEAKER "When I talk to you, I don't feel like you are really hearing what I'm saying. It seems like you roll right over me and try to make another point."

- LISTENER "I heard you say when I talk to you . . . (rephrasing as much as they can remember).
- SPEAKER "When you do that, I feel like my feelings are unimportant to you and you don't value them. How do you feel about that?"
- LISTENER "I heard you say I don't value your feelings. I feel bad that what I'm doing dishonors you and causes you to feel I don't care about your feelings. I'm sad, and I want to do something to change that dynamic. I want to learn to validate you and honor your feelings. I want to work on this together."

When this process is complete, the floor gets handed to the previous listener who becomes the speaker. Only the person who has the floor can speak. You cannot both talk at the same time. One always talks, and one always listens. Only the speaker can clarify, not the listener, unless he is repeating or paraphrasing. The speaker can pick any topic or feeling they want to discuss. They have the uncensored right to speak about whatever they want. It helps for the speaker to give the listener only small amounts of information that the listener restates in paraphrase. Start with one or two simple ideas or statements.

Don't move on to other issues until you're both satisfied you've talked through the process, and both feel heard. As you feel safer, you can explore more without needing to use a speaker-listener tool.

Whenever we get stuck in the process of talking and feel a conflict building, we stop and say, "We've stopped listening to each other. Let's use the speaker-listener exercise to make sure we don't go off the rails and unpack this without dishonoring our feelings."

When we use this tool, intensifying emotions are put in check, so they don't escalate. The structure "forces" us to listen without defending because we are concentrating on active listening, instead of defending. We are both heard, and the words, thoughts, and feelings are validated.

The Healing Power of Validation

Validation opens the heart to intimacy. When our feelings are validated— heard and understood, our hearts open up and we feel loved. That's what makes this tool so powerful; it removes our defensive, non-listening habits and helps us actively listen and then validate. The natural response to this is to open our hearts more to our spouse—the very thing we're after. This exercise is hard at first but gets easier with practice. We still use the speaker-listener tool at times when a subject is sensitive, and we try to fall back into defensive or non-listening postures.

We recognize when we are not listening to each other and stop our escalation by using this tool. We slay the escalation dragon with the three arrows of active listening, validation, and honoring feelings.

Chapter 8: Banish Shame

Connection Questions

1. Can you relate to the Prodigal Son reference from Lk 15:11-32? Take time to read that story together and talk

about where you see yourself on the road back to the father's house.

2. How do you think the father feels about you and where you are on the road? Are you open to him or closed off? Is he shepherding your heart close up, or are you holding him at arm's length?

3. Are you confident to receive God's grace and healing in your broken places, or does your shame tempt you to hide from God or your spouse? Read Heb.10:14-23 and talk.

4. How do you feel about accepting your broken places? Can you let God's grace in to heal or do you wall areas off so you can work on them without him?

Chapter 9: Heal Your Sexuality

Connection Questions

1. This chapter is about finding freedom from sexual bonds, no matter where we've been sexually. Do you believe this is possible that we can be free no matter where we've been and what's happened to us?

2. Are you willing to engage Jesus on this journey of healing your sexuality? Will you consecrate your sexuality to him and yield your body to him for purity and connection to your spouse in marriage?

3. Did the section on forgiving your past resonate with you? Are you able to forgive yourself for your past, and let the guilt and shame of it go? Is the blood of Jesus

enough for you, or will you keep punishing the old sinful you, while you try to work off your shame?

Chapter 10: Escape from Idolatry

Connection Questions

1. Did you identify with any of the marriage myths in this chapter?
2. Did you think being married would make it easier to manage your sexuality?
3. Do you have doors that may still be open to sexual sin?
4. Do you have any systems in place to help keep your walk with God pure before Him and your spouse? Like computer apps to protect you from immoral content, or accountability groups.
5. How do you handle sexual temptation—pornography or emotional dependencies? Are there any further commitments you need to make to each other to protect your marriage?

Chapter 11: Banish the Differences Myth

Connection Questions

Do you understand the language of polarization—that we've fallen in love with a romanticized version of our spouse?

1. Are you still loving this *image* of your spouse designed

to serve you? Are you still trying to change things about them to line them up with your expectations, or needs?

2. Do you still see your spouse as an obstacle to your happiness because they aren't who you *need* them to be?

3. Can you commit to accept them as they are and stop trying to change them? Verbalize this commitment to each other if you can.

Replenishers and Depleters

How do you recharge? Put a + in front of the things that make you feel replenished and a – in front of things that make you feel depleted. Have your spouse do the same. Talk about why certain things make you feel energized or drained. Compare your answers and see if your differences are creating a challenge in your marriage. Strategize together on how to meet your needs.

1. Spending time together to talk about feelings and concerns
2. Going on a drive together to a scenic place or to shop
3. Going to a movie together
4. Tackling difficult issues together
5. Going to hear live music together
6. Children's activities
7. Housework
8. Taking a walk
9. Praying together
10. Going to church
11. Reading an interesting book
12. Going to ministry meetings

13. Teaching or facilitating a class or event
14. Cooking a meal
15. Going out to dinner
16. Watching a sunset or storm
17. Throwing a party
18. Having a couple over for dinner
19. Helping or counseling another person or couple
20. Visiting relatives
21. Doing nothing structured, just hanging out and letting the day unfold
22. Other_____

Chapter 12: Wield Words Well

Connection Questions

1. What does it mean when we say our words are working for us — they are always *doing* something?
2. Do you understand relational messages, and what it means to send them? Give an example.
3. Do you sometimes let reckless words get away from you? Where can you be more intentional about how you send them?

Go through the following chart of relational messages separately. These are messages we send behind our words and attitudes that may not be said directly to their face — but they get the message. Mark areas you struggle with and talk about them. Ask your partner for life-giving words that can help you heal in areas of struggle. Tell them how you feel and what kinds of words would make you feel loved and supported. Make some commitments about words you will use in the future. Confess and forgive each other. Pray together for God to help you with your words.

DEATH-DEALING MESSAGES	LIFE-GIVING MESSAGES
You have no value.	I appreciate you.
I reject you.	I accept you unconditionally, the way you are.
I blame you; it's your fault.	I'm willing to take responsibility for my part.
You are stupid. You don't make any sense.	I may not agree, but I value your opinion.
I am better than you. My way is better.	I will treat you and your opinions equal to mine.
You are a failure. You'll never be anything.	You can do this. I believe in you.
You're a lousy father, mother, provider, etc.	You're doing the best you can. I trust you.
If you just change, our marriage would be better, and I'd be happy.	I will take responsibility to make changes in my own life.
I disapprove of you. You disappoint me.	I will lower my expectations and support you.

Chapter 13: Break the Chains of Dysfunctional Relationships

Connection Questions

Is there a specific relationship, past or present, keeping you in chains? There is a path to freedom:

1. Ask God to help you forgive. The deeper something hurts us, the harder it is to forgive. Especially if there are repeat offenses. We can say, "I forgive you," but our hearts need to heal from the damage done to us. Whether you are carrying unforgiveness toward an ex, a family member, a friend, an authority figure, or even your current spouse, ask the Lord for special grace. Tell him you want to forgive and heal.

2. Ask God for wisdom to show you how to set healthy boundaries, and maybe necessary endings. If you haven't been doing this, or don't know how, you may need someone to come alongside to help you.

3. Ask God to bring people and resources into your life to empower you to take this next step. Don't be afraid to ask for help.

4. If the toxic relationship is not with your spouse, ask your spouse to pray with you. Together, ask God to show you what you need.

Made for Love

My heart is made for love but gets attacked by hate.
I want to hang with tenderness, but bitterness wants a date.

Her kiss is naught but venom, poisoning my love,
Killing heaven's song singing from above.

Forgiveness is the arrow, piercing hatred's soul
Bleeding out the darkness, my heart's becoming whole.

Where is found this grace to have this point of view?
"Father, please forgive them; they know not what they do."

Dan Lillyblad

Chapter 14: Celebrate the Gift of Sexuality

What Can I Do Today?

1. Talk about how things are going for you as a couple sexually. Be safe and honest.
2. Discuss a strategy if you want things to change.
3. Pick one of the areas written in this chapter you need to talk about.

Chapter 15: Freedom Fighters

What Can I Do Today?

1. Which of the seven conflicts can you most identify with in your marriage?
2. Would you say you are an avoider of conflict or a bulldog who wants to go after it?
3. Share your fears or needs that you can see fueling some of your conflicts.
4. Now talk about and record a strategy you can develop to help meet those needs and reduce conflict.

Chapter 16: The Road Home

Connection Questions

1. We listed seven things on the road home that sustain us on the journey to the end. They are, Stay corporate, Agree on core values, Resolve issues, Stay positive, Keep short accounts, Stay in agreement, and Enter the emotion pool of marriage. Look at each one of these together and decide which ones are strengths and which are weaknesses. Which ones can you agree to work on? Can you create a mission statement together for your marriage? If you can do this, set a date when you will revisit it and talk about how you're doing.

Notes

Chapter 1: Someday My Prince Will Come
1. C.S. Lewis, *The Four Loves* (Inspiration Press, 1991), 274.
2. John and Stasi Eldredge, *Love and War: Finding the Marriage* You've dreamed of (Doubleday, 2009), 47–48.

Chapter 2: Life in Separate Towers
1. John and Stasi Eldredge, *Love and War*, 5.
2. Mark Gungor, Laugh Your Way to a Better Marriage: Unlocking the Secrets to Life, Love, and Marriage (Atria, 2008), 78–80.
3. John and Stasi Eldredge, Love and War: Finding the Marriage You've Dreamed Of (Doubleday, 2009), 5.
4. Larry Crabb, The Silence of Adam: Becoming Men of Courage in a World of Chaos (Zondervan, 1995), 87–99.
5. William F. Harley, Jr., *His Needs, Her Needs: Building An Affair-Proof Marriage.* Grand Rapids, Mi. Revell, 2011:), chap. 4.
6. William F. Harley, Jr., *His Needs, Her Needs*, 54–56.

Chapter 3: The Curse of Stolen Identity
1. Alex A. Avila, Three Thoughts Couple Devotional: Engaging the Power of Our Minds and Hearts to Cultivate a Lifestyle of Intimacy (Alex A. Avila, 2017), 68.

Chapter 4: Invite the Hero of Your Story into Your Quest
1. A.W. Tozer, *The Best of A.W. Tozer* (Baker, 1978), 239.

2. A.W. Tozer, The Best of A.W. Tozer, 134.
3. A.W. Tozer, A Treasury of A.W. Tozer: A Collection of Tozer Favorites (Baker, 1981), 154.
4. A.W. Tozer, A Treasury of A.W. Tozer, 152.

Chapter 5: Secure the Castle

1   Gary Smalley, I Promise: How Five Commitments Determine the Destiny of Your Marriage (Nelson, 2006), 6, 10.
2   Michael and Amy Smalley, The Surprising Way to a Stronger Marriage: How the Power of One Changes Everything (Tyndale, 2010), 6.
3   M. Scott Peck, The Road Less Traveled—A New Psychology of Love, Traditional Values, and Spiritual Growth (Touchstone, 2003), 271.
4   Dan B. Allender and Tremper Longman, Intimate Allies: Rediscovering God's Design for Marriage and Becoming Soul Mates for Life Tyndale, 1995), 117.

Chapter 6: Win the Power Challenge

1   Gordon Dalbey, *Healing the Masculine Soul, An Affirming Message for Men and the Women Who Love Them* (Word Publishing, 1988), 43.
2   Gordon Dalbey, *Healing the Masculine Soul* (Word, 1988), 59.
3   Gordon Dalbey, Healing The Masculine Soul, 42

Chapter 7: Break the Curse of "Me" over "We"

1   *The Family Man*, written by David Diamond and David Weissman, directed by Brett Ratner (Universal Studios, 2000).
2   Anne Wilson Schaef, *Meditations for Women Who Do Too Much* (Harper One, 2000).
3   Leanne Payne, The Broken Image: Restoring Personal Wholeness through Healing Prayer (Baker, 1996), 140.

Chapter 8: Banish Shame

1   Andrew Comiskey, Living Waters: Restoring Relational Integrity through the Broken Body of Christ (Desert Stream Ministries, 1996), 16.
2   Andrew Comiskey, *Living Waters*, 16.

3   Leanne Payne, The Broken Image: Restoring Personal Wholeness through Healing Prayer (Baker, 1996), 26–27.

4   Nicholas Harnan, *The Heart's Journey Home: A Quest for Wisdom* (Ave Maria Press, 1992), 61.

5   Brennan Manning, Abba's Child: The Cry of the Heart for Intimate Belonging (Navpress, 2002), 21.

6   Andrew Comiskey, Living Waters: Restoring Relational Integrity through the Broken Body of Christ (Desert Stream Ministries, 1996), 20.

7   Andrew Comiskey, *Living Waters*, 130.

Chapter 9: Heal Your Sexuality

1   Andrew Comiskey – Naked Surrender – Coming Home To Our True Sexuality – InterVarsity Press, 2010, 49

2   C.S. Lewis – The Screwtape Letters-A Devil's Diabolical Advice For The Capturing Of The Human Heart (Bantam – 1982 – 65)

3   *Family Man*, written by David Diamond and David Weissman, directed by Brett Ratner (Universal, 2000).

Chapter 10: Escape from Idolatry

1   Neil T. Anderson and Charles Mylander, The Christ Centered Marriage: Discovering and Enjoying Your Freedom in Christ Together (Regal, 1996), 179.

2   Steve Gallagher, At *the Altar of Sexual Idolatry* (Pure Life Ministries, 2000).

Chapter 11: Banish the Differences Myth

1   Notting Hill, Directed by Roger Michell, written by Roger michell and Richard Curtis, produced by Duncan Kenworthy-1999

2   Les and Leslie Parrott, Love Talk: Speak Each Other's Language Like You Never Have Before (Zondervan, 2004), 51.

Chapter 13: Break the Chains of Dysfunctional Relationships

1   Dr. Henry Cloud, Necessary Endings: The Employees, Businesses, and Relationships That All of Us Have to Give Up in Order to Move Forward (Harper-Collins, 2010), 143.

2   Danny Silk, Keep Your Love On: Connection, Communication, and Boundaries (Loving On Purpose Ministries, 2013), 72–73.

Chapter 14: Celebrate the Gift of Sexuality

1   Dr. James Dobson, *What Wives Wish Their Husbands Knew About Women* (Tyndale, 1987), 100.
2   John and Stasi Eldredge, *Captivating, Unveiling the Mystery of a Woman's Soul,* (Nelson, 2021), 41.
3   Gary Chapman, *The 5 love Languages: The Secret to Love That Lasts* (Northfield, 2015).
4   John and Stasi Eldredge, *Captivating*, 41.
5   Dan B. Allender, The Wounded Heart: Hope for Adult Victims of Childhood Sexual Abuse (NavPress, 1995).
6   Dennis and Barbara Rainey, *Rekindling the Romance* (Nelson, 2005), 70, 72.
7   Dennis and Barbara Rainey, *Rekindling the Romance*, 73.
8   Alex A. Avila, Three Thoughts Couple Devotional: Engaging the Power of Our Minds and Hearts to Cultivate a Lifestyle of Intimacy (Alex Avila, 2017), 148.
9   Gary Chapman, *The Five Love Languages* (Northfield, 2015).
10 Ed Wheat and Gloria Okes Perkins, Love Life For Every Married Couple: How to Fall in Love, Stay in Love, Rekindle Your Love (Zondervan, 1980), 76–77.
11 Dennis and Barbara Rainey, *Rekindling the* Romance, 58.
12 Gary Smalley, *For Better or Best*, 30.
13 Gary Smalley, *For Better or Best*, 30.

Chapter 15: Be a Freedom Fighter

1   Tim and Joy Downs, The Seven Conflicts: Resolving the Most Common Disagreements in Marriage (Moody, 2003).
2   Willard F. Harley Jr., His Needs, Her Needs: Building An Affair Proof Marriage (Revell, 2011).

About the Author

Daniel Lillyblad is an entrepreneur and avid weather watcher in Parker, Colorado. As a writer, he draws on personal experience as well as forty-plus years of ministry in and to the body of Christ.

He was licensed and served as a pastor in Casper, Wyoming, and later in the Cherry Creek Vineyard in Englewood, Colorado.

Dan also served in ministry at The Rock Church in Castle Rock, Colorado, for more than two decades helping develop small groups and train ministry teams. He also served several years as an elder. A licensed marriage pastor and counselor, Dan and his wife, Linda, also led retreats and classes, developed curriculum, and conducted book and video studies on marriage. He is certified with Prepare/Enrich and the SYMBIS marriage mentoring program with Les and Leslie Parrot.

In his book *The Quest for Happily Ever After*, Dan helps couples discover the hidden roots of disconnect in marriage, learn strategies to help them heal and grow, and experience the kind of deep oneness that will help them go the distance.

www.ingramcontent.com/pod-product-compliance
Lightning Source LLC
Chambersburg PA
CBHW030407130626
46549CB00004B/1661